Master the SPaG basics with CGP!

This Foundation Question Book from CGP is perfect for helping pupils aged 7-8 get to grips with English in Year 3.

It's bursting with practice questions to help pupils improve the essential grammar, punctuation and spelling skills they'll need.

Each topic starts with helpful examples and there are answers to every question at the back of the book!

What CGP is all about

Our sole aim here at CGP is to produce the highest quality books — carefully written, immaculately presented and dangerously close to being funny.

Then we work our socks off to get them out to you — at the cheapest possible prices.

Contents

Grammar

Section 1 — Word Types
Nouns 4
Adjectives 5
Articles 6
Verbs 8
Adverbs 10
Mixed Practice 12

Section 2 — Clauses, Phrases and Sentences
Clauses 14
Phrases 15
Statements and Questions 16
Commands and Exclamations 18
Mixed Practice 20

Section 3 — Conjunctions and Prepositions
Conjunctions 22
Prepositions 24

Section 4 — Verb Tenses
Present and Past Tense — Regular Verbs ... 26
Present and Past Tense — Irregular Verbs .. 28
Staying in the Same Tense 30

Punctuation

Section 5 — Sentence Punctuation
Capital Letters for Names and I 32
Capital Letters and Full Stops 34
Question Marks 36
Exclamation Marks 38
Sentence Practice 40

Section 6 — Commas
Writing Lists 42
Writing Longer Lists 44

Section 7 — Apostrophes
Apostrophes for Missing Letters 46
Its and It's 48
Apostrophes for Single Possession 50
Apostrophe Practice 52

Section 8 — Inverted Commas
Inverted Commas 54
Punctuating Speech 56

Section 9 — Paragraphs and Layout
Paragraphs 59
Headings and Subheadings 61

Contents

Spelling

Section 10 — Prefixes

Prefixes — 'un' 'dis' and 'mis' 62
Prefixes — 're' and 'anti' 64
Prefixes — 'sub' and 'super' 65
Mixed Practice 66

Section 11 — Suffixes and Word Endings

Word Endings — 'sure' and 'ture' 68
Suffixes — 'ing' and 'ed' 70
Suffixes — 'er' and 'est' 72
Suffixes — 'ful' 'less' 'ment' and 'ness' 74
Mixed Practice 77

Section 12 — Confusing Words

The short 'i' sound 79
The hard 'c' sound 80
The soft 'c' sound 81
The 'sh' sound 82
The 'ay' sound 83
Word Families 84
Plurals 85
Homophones 88
Mixed Practice 90

Glossary 92
Answers 95

Published by CGP

Editors
Zoe Fenwick, Melissa Gardner, Kelsey Hammond, Katharine Howell, Becca Lakin, Hannah Roscoe
With thanks to Alison Griffin and Emma Crighton for the proofreading.
With thanks to Jan Greenway for the copyright research.
Thumb illustration used throughout the book © iStock.com.
The Grammar and Punctuation sections contain public sector information licensed under the Open Government Licence v3.0.
http://www.nationalarchives.gov.uk/doc/open-government-licence/version/3/

ISBN: 978 1 78908 333 0

Clipart from Corel®
Printed by Elanders Ltd, Newcastle upon Tyne.
Based on the classic CGP style created by Richard Parsons.

Text, design, layout and original illustrations © Coordination Group Publications Ltd. (CGP) 2019
All rights reserved.

Photocopying this book is not permitted, even if you have a CLA licence.
Extra copies are available from CGP with next day delivery • 0800 1712 712 • www.cgpbooks.co.uk

Section 1 — Word Types

Nouns

Nouns are words that name things.

Common nouns are everyday words for things. ⟹ boat   window

Matt   Newcastle   Sunday ⟵ Proper nouns are names for particular people, places or things.

1) Draw lines to match the nouns below to the correct picture.

snake   apple   bird   spoon

2) Shade in the clouds that contain proper nouns.

banana   table   Tip: proper nouns always have a capital letter.

April   Friday

cat   Scotland   Chester

"I know what nouns are."

Section 1 — Word Types   © CGP — not to be photocopied

Adjectives

Adjectives are words that tell us **more** about a **noun**.

the blue van   a long dress   a famous person

1 Draw lines to connect each animal to three adjectives that describe it.

grey

dirty

pink

fluffy

happy

angry

2 Underline the adjective in each of the phrases below.

One has been done for you.

the spotty pants

a <u>good</u> book

a small dog

the big lizard

a hungry horse

a green door

the sad shark

the sticky floor

"I know what adjectives are and how to use them."

Articles

Articles are the words 'a', 'an' and 'the'. They go before nouns.

Use 'a' when the noun starts with a consonant sound. → I want a crayon.

She ate an orange. ← Use 'an' when the noun starts with a vowel sound.

1 Circle the articles in the sentences below.

I found an ant.

Malika has a garden.

This is an otter.

We saw a zebra.

Vowel sounds are usually made by the letters 'a', 'e', 'i', 'o' and 'u'.

2 Shade in the sentence that uses the correct article.

There is an elephant.   There is a elephant.

3 Draw lines to match the words to the correct article.

umbrella   bee

girl

a   an

        arrow

oven

rainbow   flower

Section 1 — Word Types

Use 'the' when talking about specific things.

The dog barked. ← This means a particular dog.

Use 'a' and 'an' when talking about general things.

This means any dog. → A dog barked.

4) Tick the boxes next to the phrases that use articles correctly.

the party ✓   an orange ☐   an dinosaur ☐

a eagle ☐   the day ☐   a gift ☐

5) Choose one article to fill each gap. Only use each option once.

 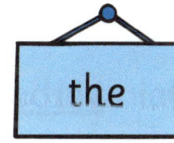 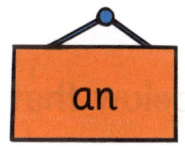 

.... owl   .... frog

6) Circle the correct article in the sentences below.

I spoke to her on <u>the</u> / <u>an</u> phone.

Thailand is <u>the</u> / <u>a</u> country in Asia.

This film is <u>the</u> / <u>a</u> best!

"I know what articles are and when to use them."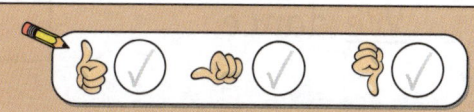

Verbs

Verbs are doing or being words.

I watch TV.   He makes cheese.   They are going.

1) Match the verbs below to the correct picture.

sing   drink   kick   jump

2) Shade in the shapes below that contain verbs.

eat   story   speak   hear

ten   sad   know

3) Tick the sentences where the underlined word is a verb.

They <u>like</u> kittens. ☐   Jena is <u>happy</u>. ☐

<u>We</u> dance. ☐   He <u>screams</u>. ☐

Section 1 — Word Types

The verb needs to match the person doing the action.

I walk home.   She walks home.   We walk home.

4) Draw lines to match each word to the correct form of the verb.

Boris   you

     play

I   the boy

     plays

they   she

5) Circle the verbs in the sentences below.

I am happy.

You listen.   We see Grandma.

Magda loves animals.   He wins the prize.

6) Circle the correct form of the verb in each of the sentences below.

He swims / swim .   We go / goes to the park.

I talk / talks to them.   He buy / buys a guitar.

She live / lives here.   She paints / paint .

"I know what verbs are and how to use them."

Adverbs

Adverbs are words that **describe verbs**.

Thalia talks loudly. ← Adverbs often end with -ly.

They can tell you **how**, **when** and **how often** the verb was done.

She fights bravely.   I arrived early.   He always argues.

1 Show which words below are <u>adverbs</u> by drawing lines to the porthole.

sadly   fish

walk   adverb   angrily

badly   usually

2 Tick the sentences where the <u>underlined</u> word is an <u>adverb</u>.

The fox moved <u>sneakily</u>. ☐

Safa <u>watched</u> carefully. ☐

We <u>practise</u> daily. ☐

The bell rang <u>suddenly</u>. ☐

Maria <u>never</u> washes up. ☐

Tick three boxes.

3) Draw lines to show whether the underlined adverb tells you how often, when or how the action was done.

The mouse moved silently.

We are leaving today.

I clean my shoes sometimes.

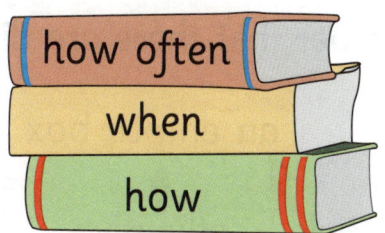

4) Underline the adverbs in the sentences below.

He skips happily.   Erin often smiles.

She always forgets.   We will go soon.

They ask nervously.   It walks slowly.

5) Complete the sentences below using the adverbs from the box.

brightly   quickly   Only use each word once.

She runs ....

The sun shines ....

"I know what adverbs are and how to use them."

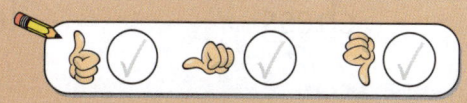

Mixed Practice

Remember that there are different types of word.

an empty box — article, adjective, noun

I smile sweetly. — verb, adverb

1) Shade the adjective that best describes the picture.

- angry
- happy
- funny

- sad
- scared
- pretty

- bad
- happy
- tired

2) Draw lines to show whether the words are verbs or nouns.

bury　　　write　　　muffin　　　lizard

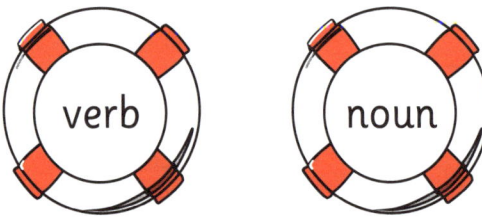

verb　　　noun

chess　　　learn　　　sandal　　　speak

Section 1 — Word Types

3 Shade the sentence that uses the correct **article**.

(I walked in a afternoon.)   (I walked in the afternoon.)

4 Complete the sentences below using the **adverbs** from the box.

(smartly   loudly   closely)

The dog growls

....

The man looks

....

The woman dresses

....

5 Complete the sentences using the correct **articles** and **nouns** to describe the picture.

articles
~~the~~   a   an

nouns
plant   ~~hat~~   umbrella

	articles	nouns
He is next to	the	....
He is wearing	....	hat ....
He is holding	....	....

"I can use different word types."

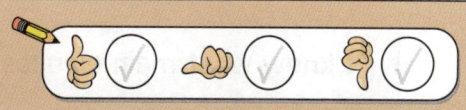

Section 2 — Clauses, Phrases and Sentences

Clauses

Most sentences are made of clauses.

A main clause makes sense on its own.

Darren cheered when his team scored.

This clause doesn't make sense on its own — it's not a main clause.

1) Tick the clauses that make sense on their own.

the girls skipped ☐   if there is time ☐

and it was dark ☐   Bella giggled ☐

2) Draw lines to join each main clause on the left to its matching clause on the right. The first one has been done for you.

He was happy — once I'd finished shopping.

I went home — until her parents arrived.

She stayed up — because it was sunny.

3) Write 'M' next to the sentence where the main clause is underlined.

<u>When I left</u>, the cat meowed. ....

<u>I will sing</u> if everyone listens. ....

We can finish it <u>after we've eaten</u>. ....

"I know what main clauses are and how to spot them."

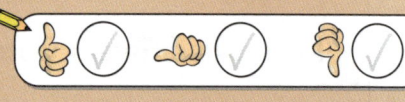

Phrases

A **phrase** is usually a group of words **without** a **verb**.

on the chair   so cold   with a smile   a brown cow

1) Shade in the groups of words that are phrases.

very smelly   next to me   I take photos   the wind blew

2) Tick the phrases that could be used to describe the picture.

a large crocodile ☐

blue and white scales ☐

really sad ☐

with a fierce grin ☐

3) Choose a phrase from the box to complete each sentence.

before the show   into tiny pieces   lemon cupcakes

Henna hid ....

The vase shattered ....

Dad ate the ....

"I can spot phrases and use them in a sentence."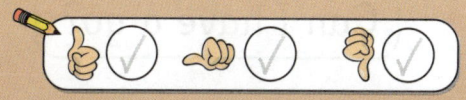

Statements and Questions

Statements tell you something. The person or thing doing the action usually comes before the verb.

The sun is shining.

thing doing the action — verb

You can turn some statements into questions by putting the person or thing doing the action after the verb.

Is the sun shining?

verb — thing doing the action

Tip: questions always end with a question mark.

1) Tick the sentences that are statements.

The first one has been done for you.

It was hot on safari. ✓

Can we have a dessert? ☐

Is the film long? ☐

The boys were shouting. ☐

I don't know where it is. ☐

Is your birthday in May? ☐

Mum's car is bright red. ☐

2) Shade in all of the boxes that contain questions.

Is someone there?   Is it strawberry?

I can't find my comb.   I am seven years old.

Can I have a go?   We're going on holiday.

3 Draw lines to match each <u>question</u> with the <u>statement</u> that answers it.

What time is it? — It is 5 o'clock.
Where is your shirt? — It's in my wardrobe.
How much is it? — It is fifty pounds.

4 Rewrite these <u>statements</u> as <u>questions</u> using the underlined words.

<u>He is</u> friendly. ➔ .... friendly?

<u>I am</u> noisy. ➔ .... noisy?

Rewrite these <u>questions</u> as <u>statements</u> using the underlined words.

<u>Are you</u> busy? ➔ .... busy.

<u>Is the soup</u> hot? ➔ .... hot.

5 Use the words from the box to write a <u>statement</u> and a <u>question</u>. Use all four words in each sentence.

is   cooking   she   pizza

Don't forget to add a question mark or full stop at the end of the sentence.

statement: ....

question: ....

"I can spot statements and questions."

Commands and Exclamations

Commands give **instructions** or **orders**. They always have a **verb** that gives an **order**. ⟶ **Shut** the door. **Be** quiet!
                               ↑   ↑
                              verb   verb

Exclamations show **strong feelings**. They start with '**How**' or '**What**'. ⟶ **How** boring this is!

(1) **Shade in all of the exclamations.**

- Wash the dirty dishes.
- How loud that music is!
- What a small kitten that is!
- Take your toys upstairs.
- What long hair you have!

(2) **Put a tick next to all of the commands.**

- Close the kitchen window. ☐
- What a lovely breeze that is! ☐
- How playful your dog is! ☐
- Take your sister to the park. ☐
- Wash your hands now. ☐
- How kind you are! ☐

3 Draw lines to match each sentence to the correct label.

How polite you are!

Put away your clothes.

What a tasty meal that was!

Stir the mixture carefully.

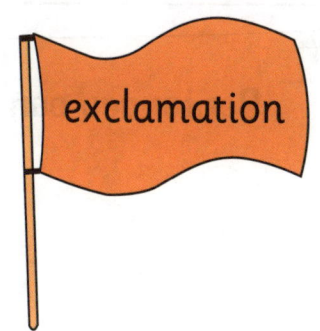

4 Read each sentence, then write the name of the person who has written an exclamation.

Jayla — Don't start without me.

Callum — What a great day it is!

Eamon — Listen to your brother.

.... has written an exclamation.

5 Use the words from the box to make one command and one exclamation.

Remember to end your sentences with a full stop or an exclamation mark.

flowers   the   water

command: ....

thirsty   am   how   I

exclamation: ....

"I can spot commands and exclamations."

Mixed Practice

Sentences can contain different types of clauses and phrases.

The lambs ran around the field.
↑ main clause   ↑ phrase

Statements, questions, commands and exclamations are all types of sentence.

1 Tick the groups of words that are phrases. The first one has been done for you.

You need to tick three more boxes.

in the way	✓	we don't agree	☐
I have a dog	☐	you aren't listening	☐
out of the box	☐	the old cleaner	☐
too salty	☐	the parrot flies	☐

2 Draw lines to match each sentence to the correct label.

Is she going to help?

I don't like vegetables.

They went to the cinema.

Why are you talking?

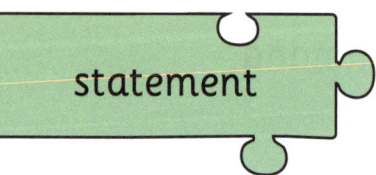

statement

question

Section 2 — Clauses, Phrases and Sentences

3) Look at the underlined words, then write down whether they're a **main clause** or a **phrase**.

I feed the chickens <u>in the morning</u>. ➡ ....

<u>We ate breakfast</u> very quickly. ➡ ....

<u>He wiped his nose</u> on his sleeve. ➡ ....

She shared the sweets <u>between us</u>. ➡ ....

They took the children <u>to the fair</u>. ➡ ....

4) Shade in the correct box to show whether each sentence is a **command** or an **exclamation**.

What lovely flowers they are!   command   exclamation

Stop chasing the rabbit.   command   exclamation

Leave the milk out for me.   command   exclamation

How exciting this is!   command   exclamation

5) Read the sentence below. Find and copy a **main clause**.

The donkey ate even though it wasn't hungry.

main clause: ....

"I can spot clauses, phrases and types of sentence."

Section 3 — Conjunctions and Prepositions

Conjunctions

Conjunctions are words or phrases that join two parts of a sentence.

She bought a flapjack, and she bought a muffin.

first part — conjunction — second part

The words for, and, nor, but, or, yet and so are all conjunctions. You can remember them using FANBOYS.

1) Shade in the four boxes that contain <u>conjunctions</u>.

- so
- five
- but
- and
- or
- walk

2) Tick the sentence that contains a <u>conjunction</u>.

You can't come inside at the moment. ☐

He didn't go outside, for it was raining. ☐

This present belongs to Amir, not Elena. ☐

3) Underline the <u>conjunctions</u> in the sentences below.

The tiger roared, so the deer ran away.

I can wash the dishes, or I can sweep the floor.

She wore blue socks with red stripes, yet no one noticed.

4 Draw lines to match the conjunctions to the correct clauses.

The rabbit ate the carrot, ➡ [and]   it was cold outside.

It had snowed, ➡ [so]   it bit my finger.

I knew it was wrong, ➡ [but]   I still stole the pencil.

5 Write the conjunction from the box in the correct place in the sentence below.

[but]

[......] I was very tired, [......] I didn't go to bed [......].

6 Use a conjunction from the balloons to complete each sentence.

 or  and  so

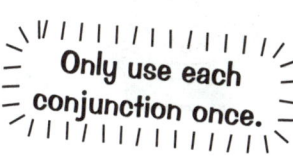 Only use each conjunction once.

The horse jumped over the gate, ... it ran away.

I will bake a cake, ... I will make a pie.

His shoes were dirty, ... he had to clean them.

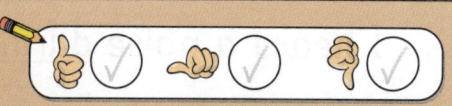
"I can use conjunctions to join sentences together."

Prepositions

Prepositions tell you **where** or **when** something happens.

I hid the present under my bed.   He watched TV at 8 o'clock.

1 Put a tick next to the sentence that matches each picture.

The hat is on Mei's head. ☐
The hat is under Mei's head. ☐

The bird is inside the tree. ☐
The bird is behind the tree. ☐

The fish is in the bowl. ☐
The fish is beside the bowl. ☐

2 Shade in the correct box to show whether the underlined preposition tells you when or where something is happening.

Jacob drew a picture after school.   when / where

Your shoes are in the hallway.   when / where

There were trees between the buildings.   when / where

I heard a noise during the night.   when / where

Section 3 — Conjunctions and Prepositions © CGP — not to be photocopied

③ **Look at the picture and read the sentences. Write the name of the person who uses the correct preposition.**

Chang — The strawberries are <u>on top of</u> the cake.

Ezekiel — The strawberries are <u>across</u> the cake.

Stevie — The strawberries are <u>in front of</u> the cake.

.... uses the correct preposition.

④ **Circle the preposition in each of the sentences below.**

The cat jumped onto the sofa.

I took some sweets from the bowl.

Nicole saw Tahani on the bus.

Please take the rubbish outside the house.

⑤ **Complete the sentences by writing a preposition on the line. Use the pictures to help you.**

The rat is .... the purse.

The bird is .... the clouds.

"I can use prepositions correctly in my sentences."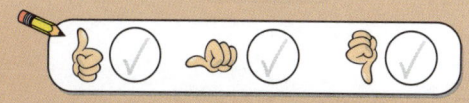

Section 4 — Verb Tenses

Present and Past Tense — Regular Verbs

Use the present tense to write about something that happens regularly.

Liam paints pictures. ← Liam does this regularly, even if he isn't doing it right now.

Use the past tense to write about something that's finished.

Lara talked to me. ← Most verbs in the past tense end in 'ed'.

1) Underline the words that are in the <u>present tense</u>.

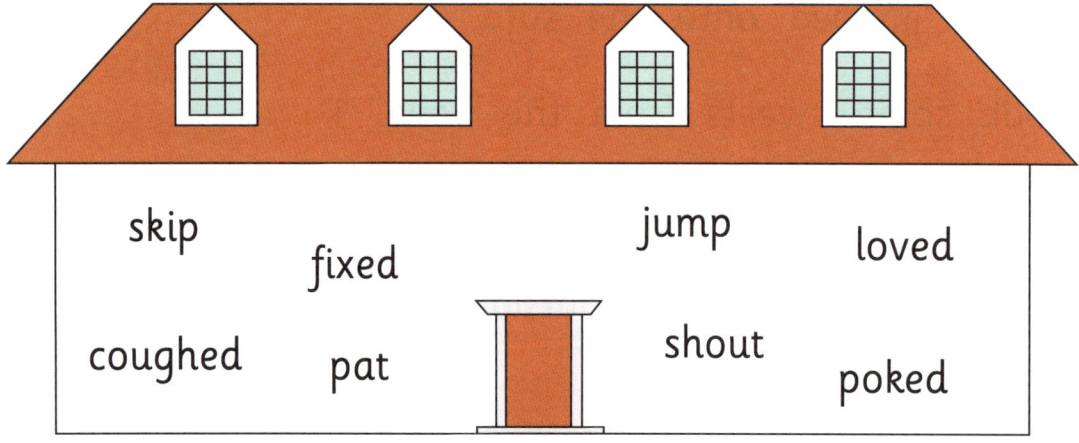

skip, fixed, jump, loved, coughed, pat, shout, poked

2) Draw lines to match each <u>verb</u> to the <u>correct</u> tense.

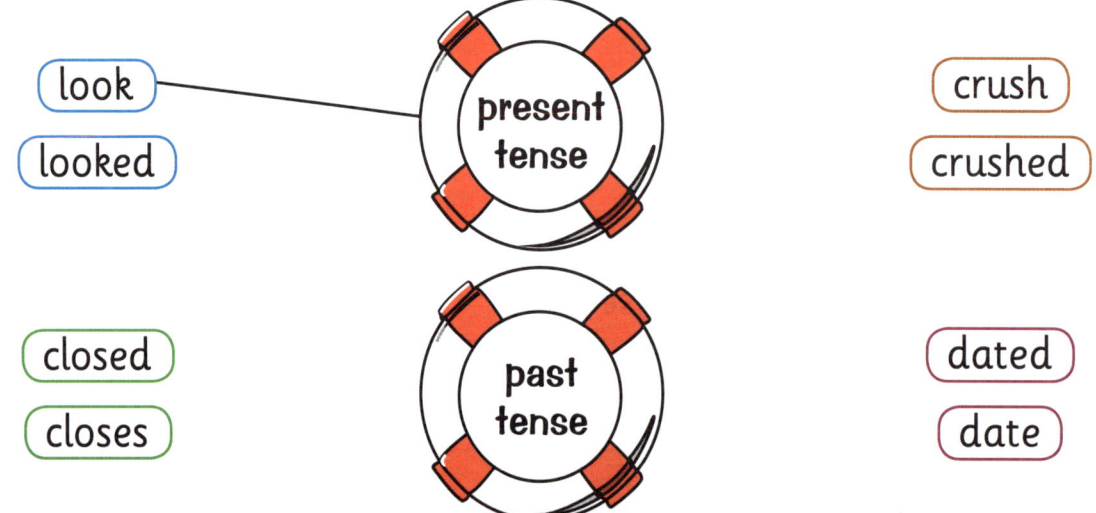

look, looked, crush, crushed, closed, closes, dated, date

present tense

past tense

3) Write the verbs in the past tense by adding 'd' or 'ed'.

use + d → used

fold + ... → ....

age + ... → ....

dress + ... → ....

4) Complete the sentences by writing the words in the boxes in the past tense.

walk — I .... my dog.

cook — Brooke .... dinner.

pick — We .... some flowers.

5) Rewrite the sentences in the past or present tense.

present tense	past tense
I chase him.	....
....	Malik cleaned.
Belle climbs.	....

"I can use regular verbs in the present and past tenses."

Present and Past Tense — Irregular Verbs

Some irregular verbs are more tricky to change into the past tense — you just have to learn these.

I eat sweets. ➡ I ate sweets.   I run fast. ➡ I ran fast.

1) Draw lines to match the present and past tense verbs.

catch   slept

makes   caught

keeps   made

sleep   kept

2) Write the missing present or past tense of the actions on the lines.

It sings.
It ....

They ....
They drank.

He sees.
He ....

She ....
She rode.

Section 4 — Verb Tenses

③ **Write the past tense form of each of these words, then find them in the wordsearch.**

have ⟶ ....

fall ⟶ ....

leave ⟶ ....

grow ⟶ ....

o	r	m	h	n	g
e	h	a	d	l	r
t	g	w	p	a	e
l	e	f	t	s	w
a	c	v	o	h	i
d	r	f	e	l	l

④ **Circle the correct spelling of the verbs in the sentences below.**

I <u>knew</u> / <u>knewed</u> it was going to rain.

Robin <u>heared</u> / <u>heard</u> the loud party.

We <u>began</u> / <u>beginned</u> our lessons.

A helicopter <u>flied</u> / <u>flew</u> over our house.

Eric <u>gived</u> / <u>gave</u> Diego a biscuit.

⑤ **Rewrite the underlined verbs using the present tense.**

I <u>rang</u> my grandma. ⟶ I .... my grandma.

Rory <u>said</u> goodbye. ⟶ Rory .... goodbye.

Fleur <u>got</u> paid. ⟶ Fleur .... paid.

"I can spot and use irregular verbs."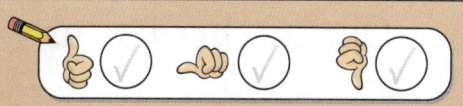

Staying in the Same Tense

The verbs in a sentence should usually be in the same tense.

I picked up the rubbish and threw it in the bin.

① Draw lines to match the beginning of each sentence to the ending that completes it.

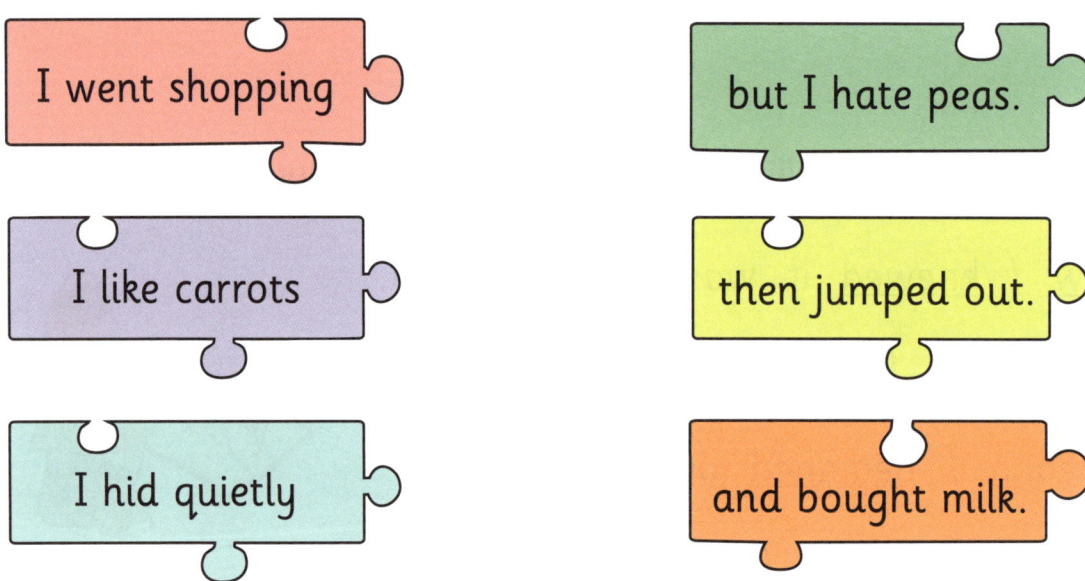

- I went shopping
- I like carrots
- I hid quietly
- but I hate peas.
- then jumped out.
- and bought milk.

② Complete the sentences by adding the verbs from the boxes.

paint   wrote   writes   painted

Only use each word once.

I chose the colours when we .... my room.

Ellie .... poetry and draws pictures.

Caleb wrapped the gift and .... in the card.

Our teacher lets us .... during art lessons.

Section 4 — Verb Tenses

3 Circle the correct form of the verbs so that each sentence stays in the same tense.

Today I visits / visited the zoo, and I saw a lion.

My mum takes / took the biscuits, and she eats them secretly.

Ajani went to the beach, and he gets / got an ice cream.

4 Rewrite the underlined verbs so that they are in the correct tense.

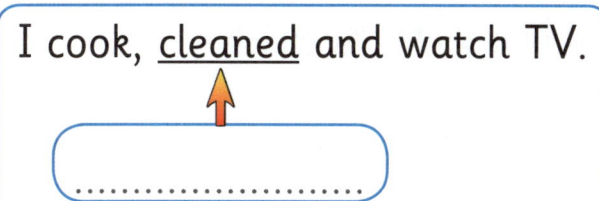
I cook, cleaned and watch TV.

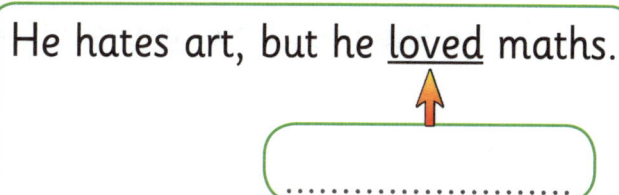
He hates art, but he loved maths.

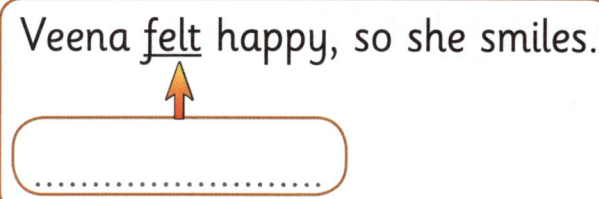
Veena felt happy, so she smiles.

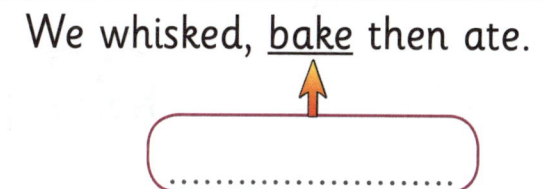
We whisked, bake then ate.

5 Add the correct verbs from the box to the passage so that it stays in the same tense.

stole / steal   goes / went

WANTED

The suspect broke into the safe and .... the diamond. Unfortunately, nobody saw where the man ....

"I can pick a tense and stick to it in my writing."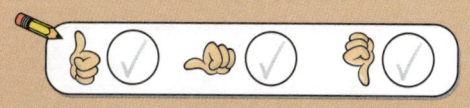

Section 5 — Sentence Punctuation

Capital Letters for Names and I

Proper nouns are the names of particular people, places or things. They always start with a capital letter.
Months, days of the week and countries all need capital letters.

Olaf   Italy   Buckingham Palace   April   Sunday

1) Draw lines to show <u>why</u> each word has a <u>capital letter</u>.

Scotland   November

Michael   Name of a person   Wales
             Name of a month
September   Name of a place   Sally

2) Circle the words in the box which should start with a <u>capital letter</u>, then write the words <u>correctly</u> on the lines.

| france | dog | katie |
| sunshine | monday | pizza |

....

....

....

3) Shade the sentence which uses <u>capital letters correctly</u>.

Norway is next to Sweden.   norway is next to sweden.

> You always need a capital letter to say "I".
>
> I lost my pen, so I looked in my bag.

4) Tick the sentence which uses capital letters correctly.

I bought a house in China. ☐

Kevin's puppy eric chewed the sofa. ☐

I got the train when i visited my sister. ☐

5) Circle the underlined words that use capital letters correctly.

My birthday is in december / December.

Eliza's favourite colour is purple / Purple.

i / I met our new neighbour called Ying.

6) Rewrite the underlined words with capital letters.

i live in cornwall. ➡ .... live in ....

It's sunny in august. ➡ It's sunny in ....

windsor castle is old. ➡ .... is old.

i saw isabelle. ➡ .... saw ....

"I can use capital letters for names and I."

Capital Letters and Full Stops

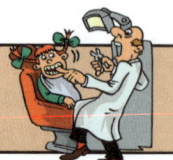

You need to start each sentence with a **capital letter**.

Sentences usually finish with a **full stop**.

The zebra is black and white.

1) Draw lines to show whether the sentences are missing a <u>capital letter</u> or a <u>full stop</u>. The <u>first</u> one has been done for you.

My pencil broke

Our plants grew

luka is late.

pass the milk.

the sun is setting.

I'm going out

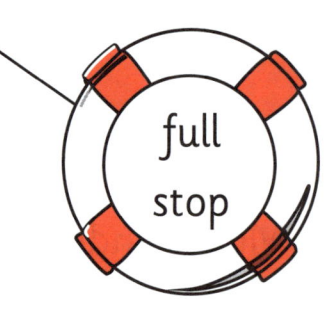

2) Add a <u>full stop</u> to the <u>correct</u> box to show where a sentence <u>ends</u>.

Haley ran a race ☐ She won a ☐ medal.

I got a ☐ new bike ☐ It is blue.

The party was ☐ fun ☐ It was loud.

I love puppies ☐ They ☐ are cute.

Tip: New sentences begin with a capital letter.

3) Circle the words in the sentence which should have a <u>capital letter</u>.

i have a dog. her name is lola. she is fluffy.

Section 5 — Sentence Punctuation

4 Rewrite the underlined words so that they start with a capital letter.

I'm very tired. i'm going to bed.
....

carrots are a vegetable.
....

pugs are nice dogs.
....

It was really cold. it snowed.
....

5 Complete the sentences with words from the boxes.

Leo / leo   .... came round to my house.

Book / book   I was reading my ....

My / my   .... football match is today.

6 Write a sentence about the picture using the words in the box.

Remember to use a capital letter and a full stop.

frog   the   wearing   is   flippers

....

....

"I can use capital letters and full stops."

Question Marks

Every **question** should end with a **question mark**.

How are you**?**   Where is the train**?**

Questions often start with **question words**. ➔ who   how   why
Here are some common ones.   what   when   where

1) Circle the question words in the box. One has been done for you.

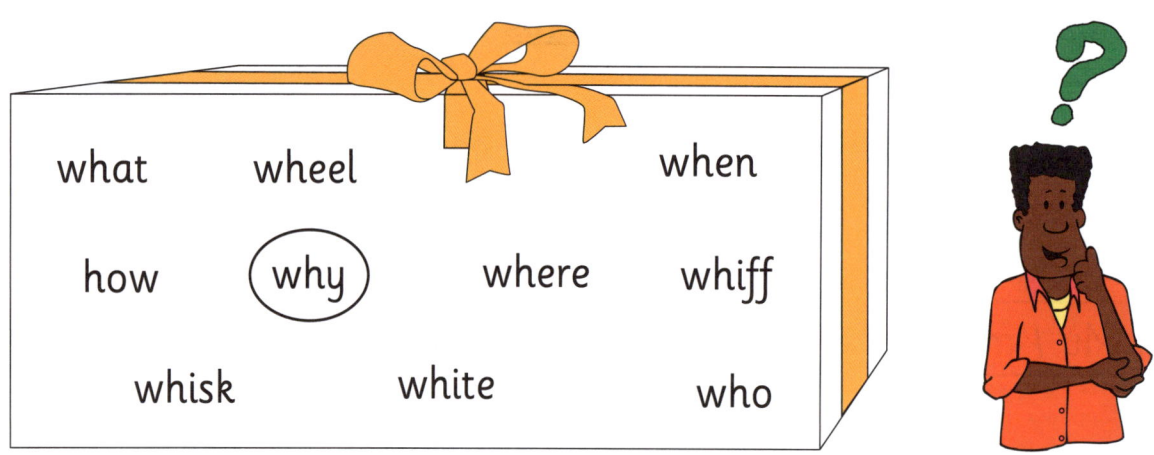

what   wheel   when
how   (why)   where   whiff
whisk   white   who

2) Tick the correct box to show if each sentence is missing a **question mark** or a **full stop**.

	full stop	question mark
What time should we leave	☐	☐
Charlie is playing a chess game	☐	☐
Tortoises have very hard shells	☐	☐
Why is everyone wearing green	☐	☐

Section 5 — Sentence Punctuation

3 Add a <u>question mark</u> or a <u>full stop</u> to the end of each sentence.

Who is that woman [?]   When are you free [ ]

My birthday is tomorrow [ ]   How was your day [ ]

Where was the party [ ]   The hamster is small [ ]

That was a nice surprise [ ]   I made a plan [ ]

4 Draw lines to show how each sentence should <u>start</u>.

... is it ready?   ... called me?

When

... did it happen?   ... can I go?

Who

... did it?   ... was there?

5 Write a <u>question</u> on the lines below to match the <u>answer</u> in the speech bubble. The first one has been done for you.

Q: .... Where is .... the hat?   A: In the box.

Q: .... is it?   A: It's 3 o'clock.

"I can use question marks correctly."

Exclamation Marks

You can sometimes finish your sentences with an exclamation mark.

Use an exclamation mark to show that something was said loudly. → "Oh no!" he shouted.

You can also use exclamation marks to show strong emotions, such as anger, fear or surprise. → The tiger has escaped!

1) Tick the sentences which use exclamation marks correctly.

The shop is giving away free sweets! ☐
The shop! is giving away free sweets ☐

They are making so much! noise ☐
They are making so much noise! ☐

2) Draw lines to match the sentences with the most likely punctuation.

Greg made a cup of tea

We are going to be so late

The sheep are in the field

All the money has been stolen

!

.

Section 5 — Sentence Punctuation

3 Add **exclamation marks** or **full stops** to the sentences.

Wow, your hair is huge .....

I like music .....

Ed is watching TV .....

Look, it's lightning .....

4 Underline the **three** sentences which are most likely to end with an **exclamation mark**.

My name is Rico

It is November

It's broken

She was horrid

I'm sleeping over

Get set, go

5 Add **one full stop** and **one exclamation mark** to the most likely place in each pair of sentences.

Yesterday was boring [.] Today was very exciting [!]

Kylie is learning Spanish [ ] It is really difficult [ ]

A gigantic storm hit the island [ ] The next day it was calm [ ]

"I can use exclamation marks correctly."

Sentence Practice

Remember that all sentences start with a capital letter, and you can use a full stop, a question mark or an exclamation mark to end them.

1) Shade in the sentences which use the most likely end punctuation.

- Where are we?
- Where are we.
- Hurry up.
- Hurry up!
- Why me!
- Why me?
- I know.
- I know?

2) Draw lines to show if the underlined words need a capital letter.

I have two <u>rabbits</u>. — no capital letter

The aliens are from <u>jupiter</u>.

Gabby likes <u>vanilla</u> ice cream.

There are mountains in <u>ireland</u>.

capital letter

3) Tick the sentences which use question marks and exclamation marks correctly.

How is it made? ☐   Get here quickly? ☐

Why are flamingos pink! ☐   The volcano is erupting! ☐

4 Underline one word in each sentence that should have a capital letter.

Nikko's family are from japan.

i rang Whitney while I was walking home.

My neighbour sheila has spiders in her porch.

Shreya received flowers for her birthday in may.

We are going on a trip to wales!

5 Circle the most likely final punctuation for the sentences.

Chloe lives in Brazil	(.)	!	?
The curry is too hot	.	!	?
Which colour would you like	.	!	?
The grass is green	.	!	?

6 Rewrite the sentence with the correct punctuation.

which one is it  ....

"I can punctuate sentences correctly."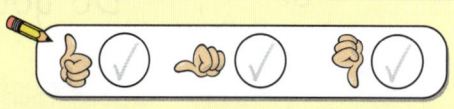

Section 6 — Commas

Writing Lists

Commas are used to separate items in a list.

I eat strawberries, apples, bananas and oranges.

You need commas between all the things in the list except the last two. You need to put 'and' or 'or' between the last two things.

1) Draw lines to match each sentence to the correct label.

- He hates cats, dogs and rabbits.
- He hates cats, dogs and, rabbits.

uses commas correctly

- She could make, pizza, pasta or soup.
- She could make pizza, pasta or soup.

uses commas incorrectly

2) Choose the correct option from the boxes below to complete the sentences.

[and] [,]   They skipped, smiled [   ] laughed.

[or] [,]   I told Jenny [   ] Niles and Wesley.

[or] [,]   Do you want water, juice [   ] squash?

3) Read the sentences below, then circle <u>one comma</u> in each sentence that <u>isn't</u> needed.

Shall we order , burgers , chips or ice cream?

The weather is clear , sunny and , hot.

The zoo , has elephants , tigers and monkeys.

4) Shade in the list that uses commas <u>correctly</u>.

I play tennis, rugby, football and hockey.

I play, tennis rugby, football and hockey.

5) Each of these sentences is <u>missing</u> one comma. Add <u>one comma</u> to each sentence to make it correct.

We need ☐ pens ☐ pencils and rubbers.

The farmer owns pigs ☐ sheep and ☐ goats.

Amira isn't ☐ greedy ☐ mean or nasty.

6) Complete the <u>list</u> below using the words from the <u>boxes</u>.

ducks   cows   pigs

We saw .... , ... and ....

"I can use commas to separate items in a list."

Writing Longer Lists

Sometimes you use several words to write about each thing in a list.

> I stroked an old donkey, two grey ponies and some lambs.

You still need to put a comma between each thing in the list and 'or' or 'and' between the last two items.

1) Put a tick in the box next to the sentences which use commas correctly.

- We sold the sparkly, shoes, the gold tiara and the dress. ☐
- We sold the sparkly shoes, the gold tiara and the dress. ☐

- He found a broken watch, a pair of gloves and a wallet. ☐
- He found a broken, watch a pair of gloves and a wallet. ☐

2) Circle one incorrect comma in each of the lists below.

- There were yellow daffodils , red tulips and white daisies , in her garden.

- They peeled the potatoes , chopped the carrots and , crushed the garlic.

- I went swimming with Felix , played netball and rode , my bike.

Section 6 — Commas

3) Read these sentences, then write the name of the person who uses <u>commas correctly</u>.

Agnes — I ate a bacon, sandwich a muffin and an ice lolly.

Kabir — I took my beach ball, my green spade and my sun hat.

.... uses commas correctly.

4) Each of these sentences is missing one <u>comma</u>. Add one <u>comma</u> to each sentence to make it correct.

I don't watch TV ☐ listen to ☐ music or play games.

She gave me ☐ some biscuits ☐ a jar of jam and a box of eggs.

I want chocolate buttons ☐ jelly beans ☐ and gummy bears.

The shop had no red grapes ☐ green peppers ☐ or brown bread.

5) The list below is missing <u>one comma</u>. Use the pictures to help you add the comma in the <u>correct place</u>.

cowboy hat   red belt   loaf of bread

She bought a cowboy hat a red belt and a loaf of bread.

"I can use commas to separate long items in a list."

Section 7 — Apostrophes

Apostrophes for Missing Letters

Apostrophes are used to show where letters are missing from a word.

I will → I'll   she is → she's   we have → we've

1) Shade in the clouds that have used apostrophes correctly.

2) Match the word pairs to their shortened versions.

Sometimes the shortened word doesn't quite match the words it's made from.

will not ➡ won't

3) Cross out the letters that will be replaced by an apostrophe. Then write the shortened word on the line.

d i d   n o t   ➡   ....

w a s   n o t   ➡   ....

t h a t   i s   ➡   ....

i t   w i l l   ➡   ....

4) Write out the underlined word in each sentence as two words.

Mum said, "We're having pie tonight."

....

"I don't like pie," said Ayana.

....

5) Shorten these words using an apostrophe.

You need to replace the underlined letters.

has n<u>ot</u> ....   does n<u>ot</u> ....

she <u>ha</u>d ....   they <u>a</u>re ....

"I can use apostrophes to shorten words."

Its and It's

The words 'its' and 'it's' mean two different things:

its ➡ This means 'belonging to it'. ➡ The cat drank its milk.

it's ➡ This means 'it is' or 'it has'. ➡ It's time for tea.

1) Tick the sentences where the underlined word means 'it is'.

It's sunny. ✓   The ant carried its food. ☐

It's Friday. ☐   It's almost Christmas. ☐

It's rained. ☐   It's red and white. ☐

It's been fun. ☐   The bird flapped its wing. ☐

2) Shade the sentence where the underlined word means 'belonging to it'.

It's worked before. | The shop closed its doors. | It's fine.

3) Write the shortened version of the underlined words on the line.

It is dark.   ➡   .... dark.

It has snowed.   ➡   .... snowed.

It is Tuesday.   ➡   .... Tuesday.

4 Put a tick next to the sentences which are punctuated correctly.

It's very cold outside. ☐

Its very cold outside. ☐

The puppy wagged its tail. ☐

The puppy wagged it's tail. ☐

5 Draw a line to match each sentence to 'it is' or 'it has'.

it is

It's been lovely.

It's raining.

It's pretty.

It's fallen over.

it has

6 Choose the correct word from the box to complete these sentences.

Its / It's …It's… three o'clock in the afternoon.

its / it's The cat carried the kitten in ………… mouth.

its / it's The bear sleeps in ………… cave.

its / it's Thank you, ………… just what I wanted.

"I can use the words 'its' and 'it's' correctly."

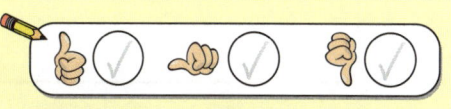

Apostrophes for Single Possession

An **apostrophe** and **'s'** shows that something **belongs**.

Nya's purse ⬅ This means **the purse belongs to Nya**.

1) Add an <u>apostrophe</u> and <u>'s'</u> to these words to show that something <u>belongs</u>.

Fiona ➕ jumper ➡ Fiona **'s** jumper.

Dad ➕ name ➡ Dad ☐ name.

The boy ➕ room ➡ The boy ☐ room.

The snake ➕ scales ➡ The snake ☐ scales.

2) Fill in the gaps in the sentences below. Remember to use an <u>apostrophe</u> and an <u>'s'</u> to show that something <u>belongs</u>.

Use the pictures to help you.

I have a book. — Sandy

It's .... book.

I have a cat. — Esme

It's .... cat.

If a name ends in an 's' already, you still need to add an **apostrophe** and an 's'. ⟶ Francis's book

This rule is the same for any **noun** ending in 's'. ⟶ the rhinoceros's horn

3 Tick the five phrases which use <u>apostrophes correctly</u>.

Carys's lemons ☐   Taylor's pencil ☐

Audreys day ☐   the class' teacher ☐

Charl'es shop ☐   Angus's cousin ☐

Eric's holiday ☐   the boss's office ☐

4 Write down what <u>each person has</u> using an <u>apostrophe</u> and an '<u>s</u>'.

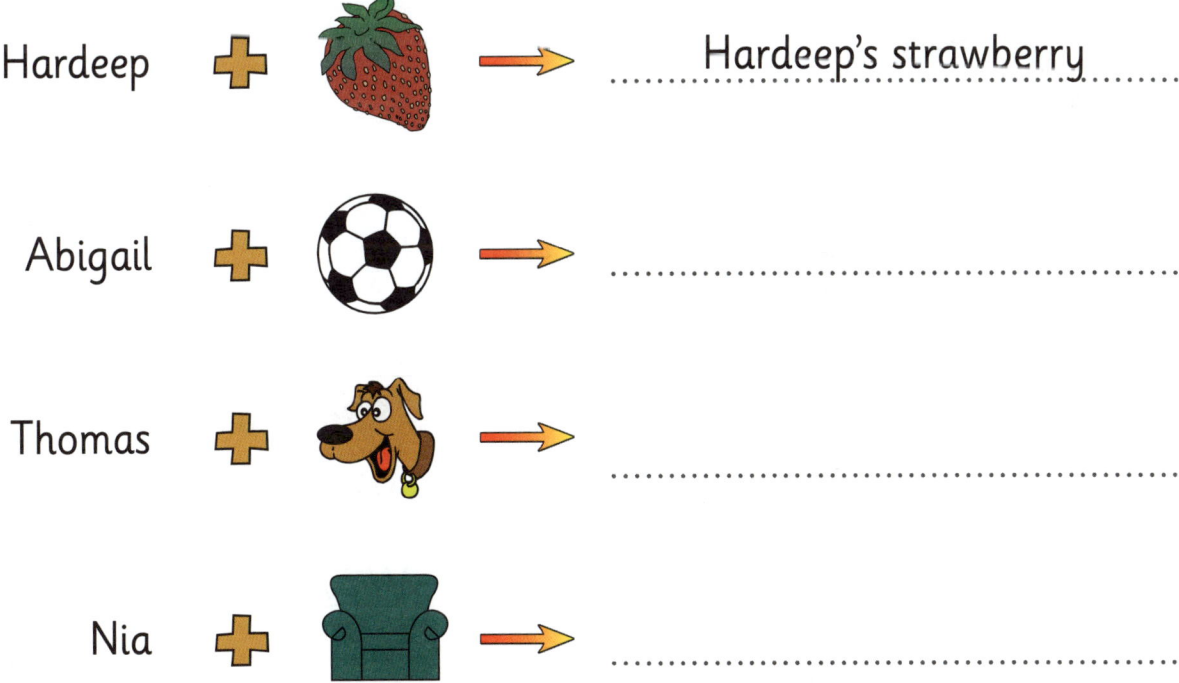

Hardeep + 🍓 ⟶ Hardeep's strawberry

Abigail + ⚽ ⟶ ....

Thomas + 🐕 ⟶ ....

Nia + 🪑 ⟶ ....

"I can use apostrophes to show something belongs."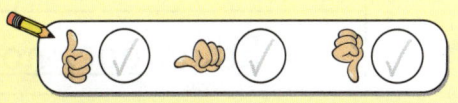

Apostrophe Practice

Remember that apostrophes can be used to show where letters are missing from a word, or to show that something belongs.

you'll ← This means 'you will'.   Ed's pen ← A pen belongs to Ed.

1) Put apostrophes in the correct places below to show that something belongs.

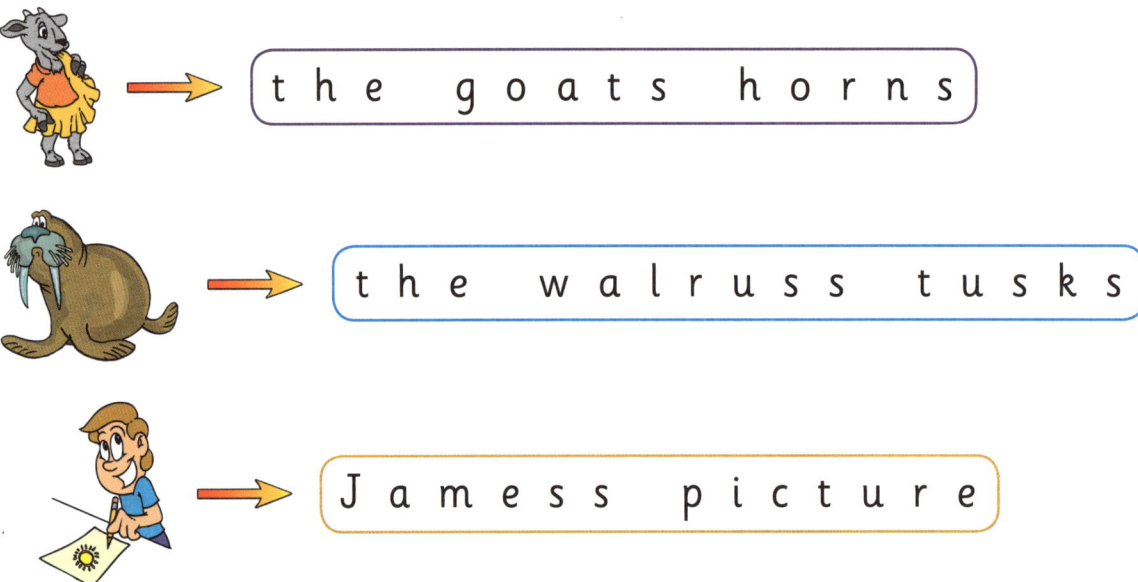

the goats horns

the walruss tusks

Jamess picture

2) Complete the table using the long and short versions of the underlined words.

Long version	Shortened version
<u>Where is</u> the party?	**Where's** the party?
.... been outside.	<u>We've</u> been outside.
<u>I am</u> Rina.	.... Rina.
.... a loud noise.	<u>That's</u> a loud noise.
Ethan <u>does not</u> shout.	Ethan .... shout.

Section 7 — Apostrophes

3) Put a cross next to the sentence which uses an apostrophe incorrectly.

Gwen's good at knitting. ☐   The mans' shoes are brown. ☐

It's time you met him. ☐   Don't do that again! ☐

4) Draw lines to show why the underlined words need an apostrophe.

for missing letters

Esther can't go

Noah's brother

the girl's eyes

we'll see you

to show possession

5) Shade in the phrase that uses an apostrophe correctly.

Naomis' game   Louis's pen   Giselles hair

6) Fill in the sentences using either 'its' or 'it's'.

.... really scary.

.... fur is purple.

.... got big feet.

"I can use apostrophes correctly."

Section 7 — Apostrophes

Section 8 — Inverted Commas

Inverted Commas

Inverted commas show when someone is speaking. They are also called speech marks.

Inverted commas go at the start and end of the speech.

"It's my turn," said Eva.

There's always a punctuation mark before the final speech marks.

'said' doesn't need a capital letter.

1) Write the name of the person who uses inverted commas correctly.

- Betty — "I like" sausages.
- Leon — "I have two brothers."
- Aoife — My dad is "called Neil".

.... uses inverted commas correctly.

2) These sentences have too many inverted commas. Cross out one incorrect inverted comma in each sentence.

" This is delicious! " said Nadine ".

" Where is the ball? " " asked Romeo.

" Come back " later, " said Zehra.

" Thank you! " said Harry. "

"Is that " the time? " asked Laurie.

3) Put a tick in the boxes next to the sentences that use inverted commas correctly.

"I want to be a teacher," said Dan. ☐

"Shall we share"? asked Elizabeth. ☐

"I play the trumpet! said" Bao. ☐

"Would you like a biscuit?" asked Alvin. ☐

4) Add the inverted commas in the correct boxes to punctuate the sentences below. The first one has been done for you.

["] Where are [ ] we going? ["] asked Daisy.

[ ] It's a lovely [ ] day, [ ] said Ansh.

[ ] I don't want to go to bed! [ ] said Damien. [ ]

[ ] There are fish in the river, [ ] said [ ] Siobhan.

5) Complete the sentences by adding the speech and the speaker.

Kat: Goodbye! → "………………………………" said ………… .

Sam: What time? → "………………………………" asked ………… .

"I can use inverted commas at the start of sentences."

Punctuating Speech

Inverted commas go at the start and end of the speech.
The first word that is spoken always has a capital letter.

"I like your new hat," she said.   Rik said, "Let's play a game!"

1 Draw lines to show if the sentence is missing an inverted comma or a capital letter.

What shall we eat?"   "how do you feel?"

"it's getting late."   Laura is ill today."

"The film was great!   "hide quickly!"

inverted comma

capital letter

2 Tick the sentences where the underlined words need a capital letter.

"do you have a middle name?" asked Sheng. ☐

Jon said, "I'd like to go on a holiday." ☐

"we don't know where we are!" cried Livia. ☐

Chase asked, "Is there room for me too?" ☐

3 Rewrite the underlined words so they use capital letters correctly.

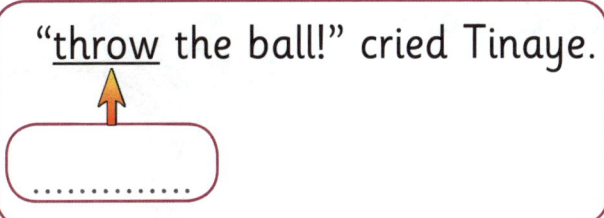

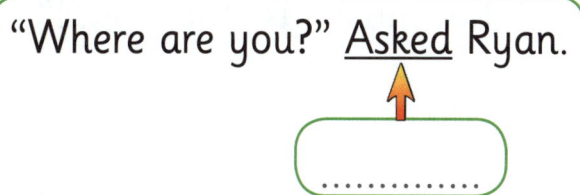

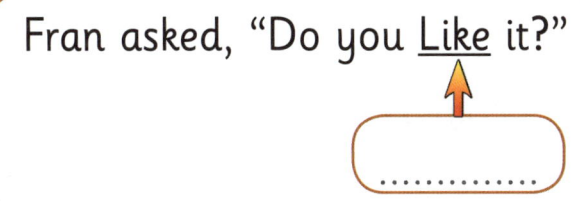

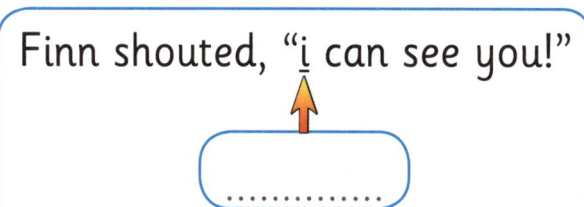

4 Complete the sentences by adding the words from the box.

have   well   whales

Remember to give the words a capital letter.

"........................ live in the sea," said Omari.

Libby said, "........................ done everyone!"

"........................ you seen my glasses?" asked Pat.

5 Shade the sentences which use inverted commas correctly.

"I'm learning how to knit! said Eugene.

"We are getting a new pet," said Tory.

Finland is "cold in the winter!" said Ingrid.

"I get my pocket money soon," said Nisha.

6 Circle the word in each sentence which needs a capital letter.

"the music is too loud!" shouted Jia.

Cameron said, "please close the door."

"i want to play the guitar," said Ariana.

7 Rewrite the sentences using inverted commas and capital letters.

Tip: The speech is underlined for you.

you're welcome, I said. ⟹ "You're welcome," I said.

Lee cried, they're here! ⟹ ....

how many? I asked. ⟹ ....

8 Tick the sentences where the speech is punctuated correctly.

"Do you want to stay over?" asked Eshal. ☐

Holly said, "I'm moving to the seaside!" ☐

"I cycle to work every day, said" Dylan. ☐

Alice asked, "Have you washed my top?" ☐

Rewrite the incorrect sentence with correct punctuation below.

....

"I can use inverted commas and capital letters to punctuate speech."

Section 8 — Inverted Commas

Section 9 — Paragraphs and Layout

Paragraphs

Paragraphs are groups of sentences that are about the same:

time   person   subject

Grouping ideas together like this makes your writing easier to read.

You can show a new paragraph by starting a new line and leaving a space.

1) Shade in the three statements about paragraphs that are true.

- They start on a new line.
- They group sentences about the same things together.
- You shouldn't use them.
- They need a new page.
- You never need to start a new paragraph.
- They make your writing easier to read.

2) Tick the correct reasons for starting a new paragraph.

When you write about a different subject. ✓   *The first one has been done for you.*

Whenever you want. ☐

When you write about a different time. ☐

When you think it will look nice. ☐

When you write about a new person. ☐

When you have written ten lines. ☐

3) Draw lines to match the sentences that could belong to the same paragraphs.

| I made a necklace at the weekend. | I really hope it doesn't rain. |
| We are going on holiday next week. | The beads are red and purple. |

4) Circle the reason why each group of sentences belong together in a paragraph.

I love dogs. They're very friendly and soft. My dog is called Spot.

time / subject

My sister is three years older than me. She has brown hair and green eyes.

person / subject

5) The following passage should have two paragraphs. Put in a paragraph marker (//) to show where the new paragraph should start.

I want to be a doctor when I grow up. I want to help make people better. My brother is a doctor. He works in a hospital.

Circle the reason for starting the new paragraph.

new time   new subject   new person

"I know when to start a new paragraph."

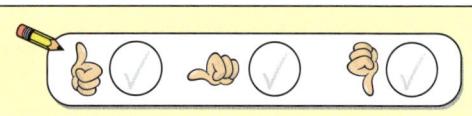

Headings and Subheadings

Headings and subheadings make text clearer and easier to read.

Headings tell the reader the main topic of the text.

Subheadings divide up the text into smaller sections.

1 Read each sentence, then write the name of the person who is correct.

Chelsea — You can only ever have one subheading on a page.

Henry — You use different subheadings for different sections.

Tariq — Subheadings make your writing harder to read.

.... is correct.

2 Draw lines to match each label to the correct part of the text below.

main text

heading

subheading

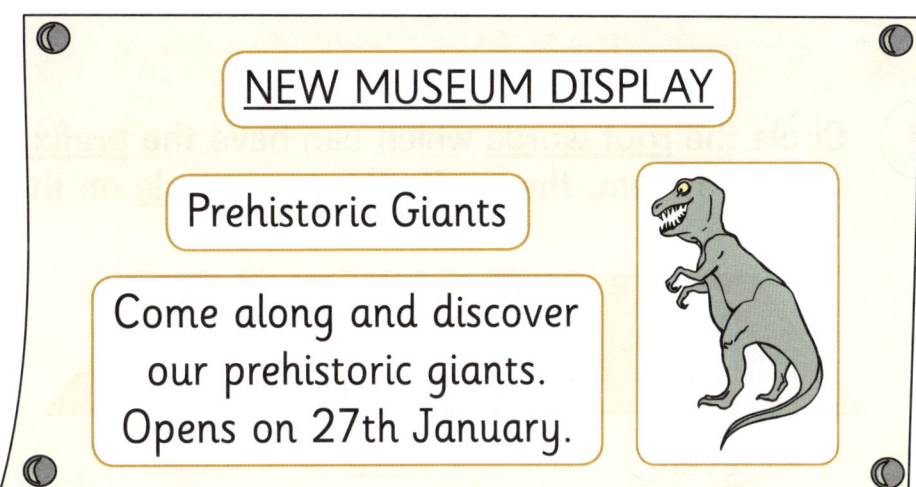

"I know when to use headings and subheadings."

Section 10 — Prefixes

Prefixes — 'un' 'dis' and 'mis'

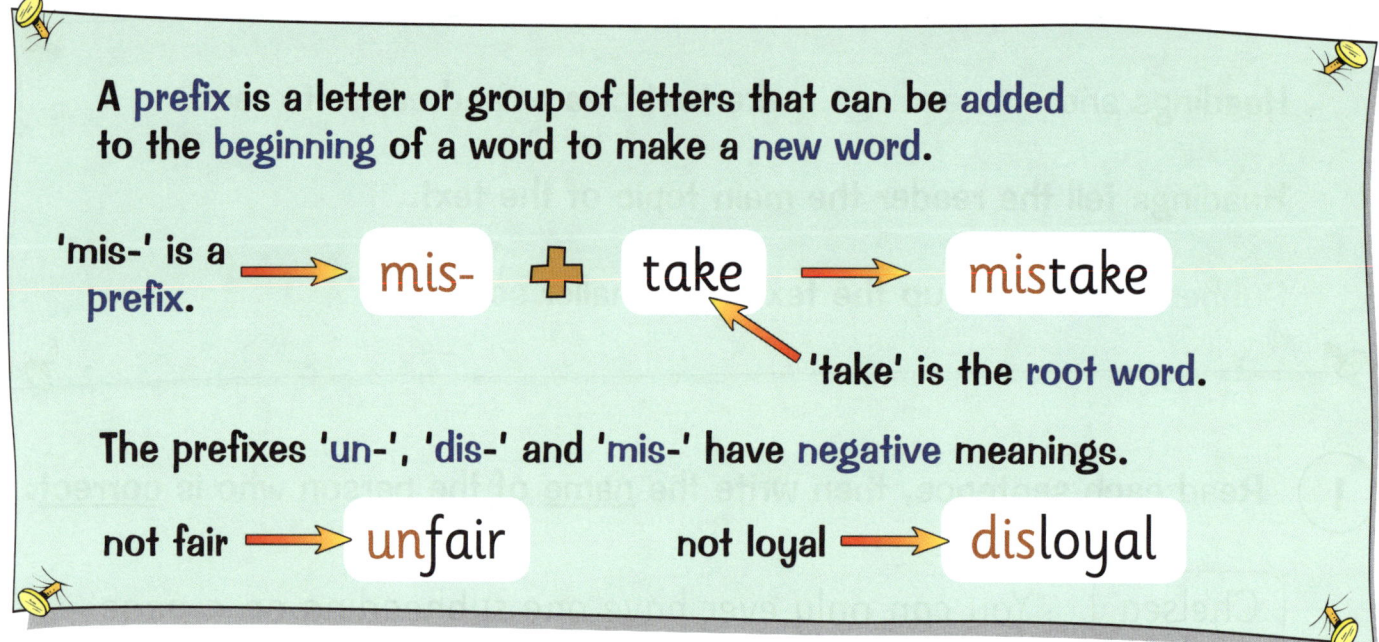

A **prefix** is a letter or group of letters that can be **added** to the **beginning** of a word to make a **new word**.

'mis-' is a prefix. → mis- + take → mistake

'take' is the **root word**.

The prefixes 'un-', 'dis-' and 'mis-' have **negative** meanings.

not fair → unfair   not loyal → disloyal

1) Draw lines to **match** the **root words** with the **correct prefix**.

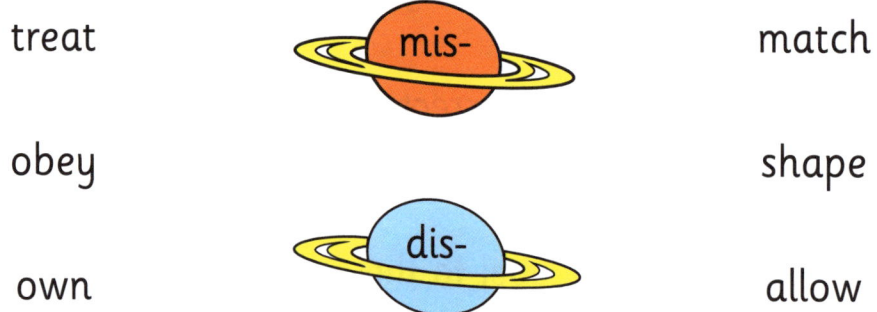

treat   mis-   match
obey   shape
own   dis-   allow

2) Circle the **root words** which can have the **prefix un-** added to them, then write the **new words** on the lines.

The first one has been done for you.

even, use, prove, play, kind, true

..........uneven..........

....

....

3 Complete the table by adding the prefixes and root words together to make new words.

Prefix	Root word	New word
dis-	grace	disgrace
un-	well	....
mis-	time	....
un-	made	....

4 Add the prefixes from the box to the correct root word.

mis- un- dis-

Use each prefix once.

..........agree

..........read

..........wrap

5 Complete the words in the sentences by adding the root words from the boxes.

approve   printed   tidy

Raheem's bedroom is un........................ .

I dis........................ of the new rules.

The newspaper mis........................ my name.

Prefixes — 're' and 'anti'

The prefix 're-' means 'again' or 'back'.

remake ← 'remake' means 'to make again'.

The prefix 'anti' means 'not' or 'against'.

'anticlockwise' means 'not clockwise'. → anticlockwise

1 Shade in the words that use the <u>correct prefix</u>.

to play again
- replay
- antiplay

not social
- resocial
- antisocial

against viruses
- antivirus
- revirus

to start again
- antistart
- restart

2 Add <u>re-</u> or <u>anti-</u> to each word, then find the completed words in the <u>wordsearch</u>.

- ..anti.. biotic
- ………climax
- ………fill
- ………view

r	x	a	e	t	r	x	t	m	i
a	r	e	v	i	e	w	w	a	f
x	n	i	r	b	f	i	w	x	e
a	n	t	i	b	i	o	t	i	c
i	b	r	w	n	l	b	e	r	b
a	n	t	i	c	l	i	m	a	x

Section 10 — Prefixes

Prefixes — 'sub' and 'super'

The prefix 'sub-' means 'under'.

submarine ← 'submarine' means 'under the sea'.

The prefix 'super-' means 'above' or 'more than'.

superhuman ← 'superhuman' means 'more than human'.

1) Unscramble the letters to make words that describe the pictures, then write the words on the lines.

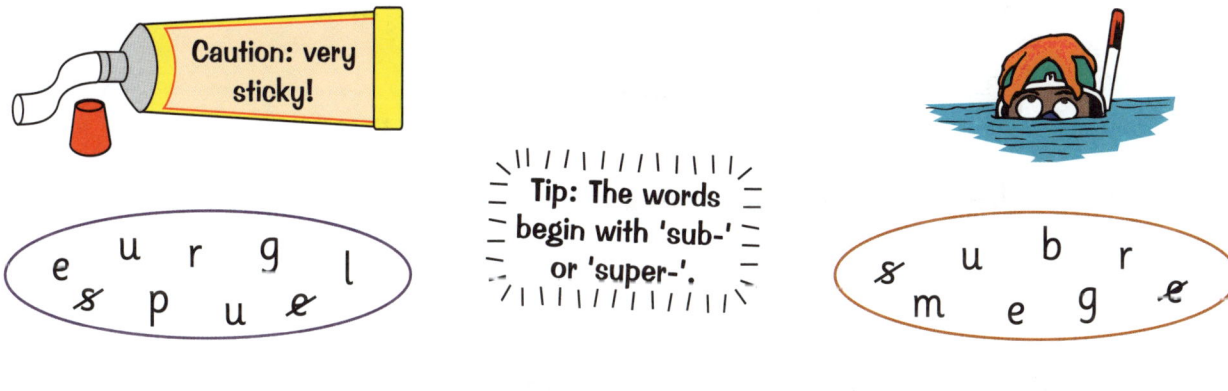

Tip: The words begin with 'sub-' or 'super-'.

s _____ e

s _____ e

2) Draw lines to match the root words to the correct prefix.

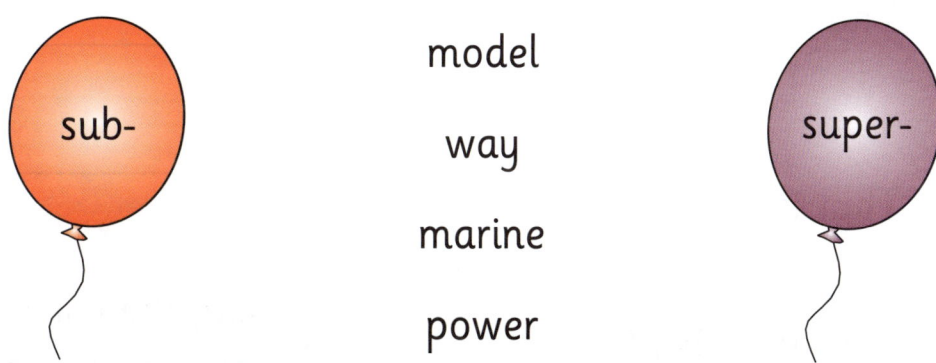

sub-   model   super-
         way
         marine
         power

Mixed Practice

Remember that a prefix is added to the beginning of a root word to make a new word.

The prefixes all have different meanings.

negative meanings			again	against	under	more than
un	dis	mis	re	anti	sub	super

1. Add the prefixes and root words together to make new words.

re- ➕ fund ➡ ....refund..........

anti- ➕ septic ➡ ....

re- ➕ place ➡ ....

anti- ➕ freeze ➡ ....

2. Write the name of the person who is using the correct prefix in the underlined words.

Tai — I have to <u>return</u> soon.

Rav — I have to <u>disturn</u> soon.

➡ .... is using the correct prefix.

Lori — That is <u>subhelpful</u>.

Kelly — That is <u>unhelpful</u>.

➡ .... is using the correct prefix.

Section 10 — Prefixes

3) Put a <u>cross</u> next to the sentence where the <u>underlined</u> word uses an <u>incorrect prefix</u>.

I <u>misheard</u> him because it was noisy. ☐

The team are <u>antibeaten</u> this year. ☐

It flew by at <u>supersonic</u> speed. ☐

4) Add the <u>correct prefix</u> from the <u>box</u> to the <u>words</u> in the sentences.

mis- / re-   I never .... behave in lessons.

super- / dis-   My last biscuit has .... appeared.

sub- / un-   There are two .... headings in the article.

5) Draw lines to match the <u>prefixes</u> to the <u>root words</u>, then write the <u>new words</u> under the <u>correct picture</u>.

Use each prefix once.

super-   un-   dis-

happy   order   hero

....

Section 11 — Suffixes and Word Endings

Word Endings — 'sure' and 'ture'

The endings '-sure' and '-ture' sound similar, but are spelt differently.

leisure   feature

1 Draw lines from the beginnings of the words to -sure or -ture.

compo-   -sure   depar-

sculp-   -ture   expo-

2 Circle the word beginnings that can have -ture added to them. Write the complete words on the lines.

mois- (circled)
sec-
cat-
mop-
fu-
pic-

.......mois.......ture

................ture

................ture

3 Unscramble the letters to make words ending -sure or -ture.

a r m t u e → m _ _ _ r _

r e t s a u r e → t r _ a _ _ _ e

4) Rewrite the incorrectly spelt words. Each word should end with -sure or -ture.

The lion's enclo<u>ture</u>.
....

It's a scary crea<u>sure</u>.
....

The struc<u>sure</u> was huge!
....

We go to the lei<u>ture</u> centre.
....

5) Complete the sentences by adding -sure or -ture to the word beginnings.

There are two words ending in -sure.

It's a plea............ to meet you!

We are buying furni............ .

She's going on an adven............ .

Let's mea............ your height.

6) Complete the sentences using the correct spellings of the words.

mixsure / mixture — She stirred the ....

nasure / nature — Cruz got a book about ....

Suffixes — 'ing' and 'ed'

A **suffix** is a letter or group of letters that can be **added** to the **end** of a word to make a **new word**.

'drink' is the **root word**. → drink + -ing → drinking

'-ing' is the **suffix**.

Sometimes the spelling of the **root** word **doesn't change** when the suffixes '-ing' and '-ed' are added.

1) Complete the table by adding -**ing** and -**ed** to the **root words**.

Root word	Add -ing	Add -ed
jump	jumping	....
hook	....	hooked
peek	....	....
fix	fixing	....

2) Add the **suffixes** to the **root words** to make **new words**, then add them to the **correct step** in the recipe.

boil + -ing → ....

mix + -ed → ....

1. Stir until the ingredients are .... together.

2. Make sure the water is ....

Sometimes the spelling of the root word changes when the suffixes '-ing' and '-ed' are added.

The 'y' in 'carry' changes to 'i'.

carry + -ed → carr**i**ed

3 Shade in the correctly spelt words below.

tidy
(tidied) (tidyed)

spot
(spotted) (spoted)

scrape
(scrapeing) (scraping)

save
(saveing) (saving)

4 Complete the sentences using the correctly spelt word from the box.

(boring / boreing)   The film was ....

(copyed / copied)   Peter .... my homework!

(tripped / triped)   He .... over his shoelace.

5 Unscramble the letters to find the root word plus a suffix.

flip

i p f g
l n i p

....

bury

e r
d b
i u

....

Suffixes — 'er' and 'est'

Sometimes the spelling of the root word doesn't change when the suffixes '-er' or '-est' are added.

'teach' is the root word. → teach + -er → teacher

'-er' is the suffix.

1) Fill in the gaps by adding the suffixes -er or -est to the root words.

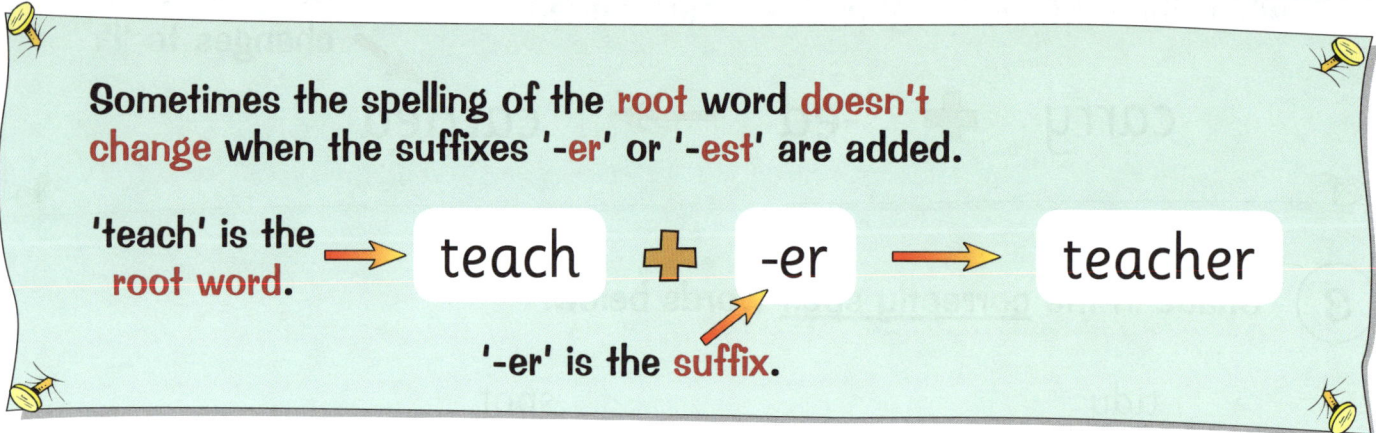

light → light...er...
loud → loud..........
great → great..........

light → light...est...
loud → loud..........
great → great..........

2) Add -er and then -est to the root words to show the sequences in the pictures.

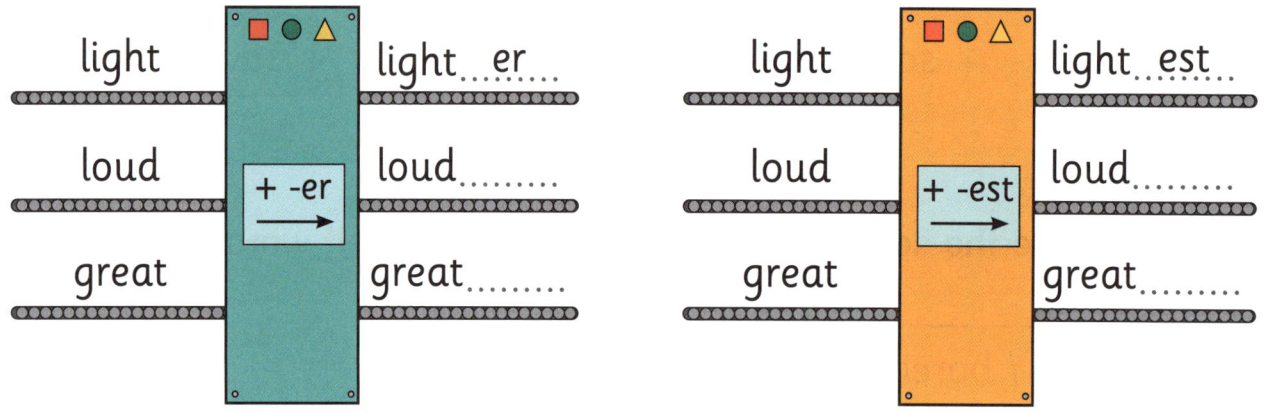

short → short.......... → short..........

long → long.......... → long..........

Section 11 — Suffixes and Word Endings

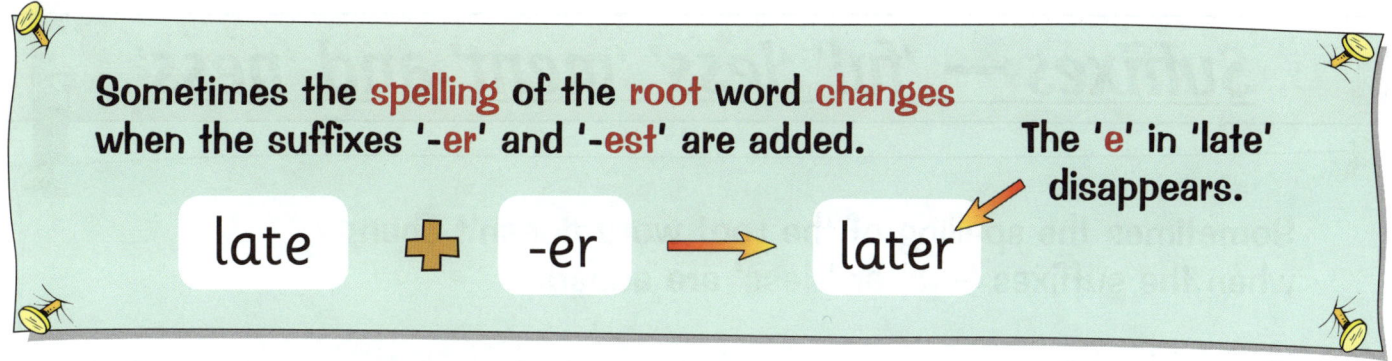

Sometimes the spelling of the root word changes when the suffixes '-er' and '-est' are added. The 'e' in 'late' disappears.

late + -er → later

③ **Circle the underlined words that are spelt correctly below.**

The dog is <u>friendlier</u> / <u>friendlyer</u> than the cat.

I am a very safe <u>driveer</u> / <u>driver</u>.

Lorenzo's costume was the <u>creepiest</u> / <u>creepyest</u>.

④ **Add the suffixes to the root words to make new words.**

The root words will change when you add the suffixes.

close → -er closer | -est ....

crazy → -er .... | -est craziest

thin → -er .... | -est ....

⑤ **Rewrite the underlined words correctly in the spaces below.**

She is a police <u>officeer</u>. → She is a police ....

I want a <u>fancyer</u> hat. → I want a .... hat.

Suffixes — 'ful' 'less' 'ment' and 'ness'

Sometimes the spelling of the root word doesn't change when the suffixes '-ful' or '-less' are added.

'power' is the root word. → power + -ful → powerful

'-ful' is the suffix.

1) Unscramble the letters in each ring to find a root word. Add the suffixes -ful and -less to each word to make two new words.

root word — new words

Ring 1: e, s, u → use → ....ful / ....less

Ring 2: e, h, l, p → .... → .... / ....

Ring 3: m, a, h, r → .... → .... / ....

2) Complete each sentence with the correct root word from the box.

The painting looked ....less.

The quiet park was ....ful.

Box: peace, flaw

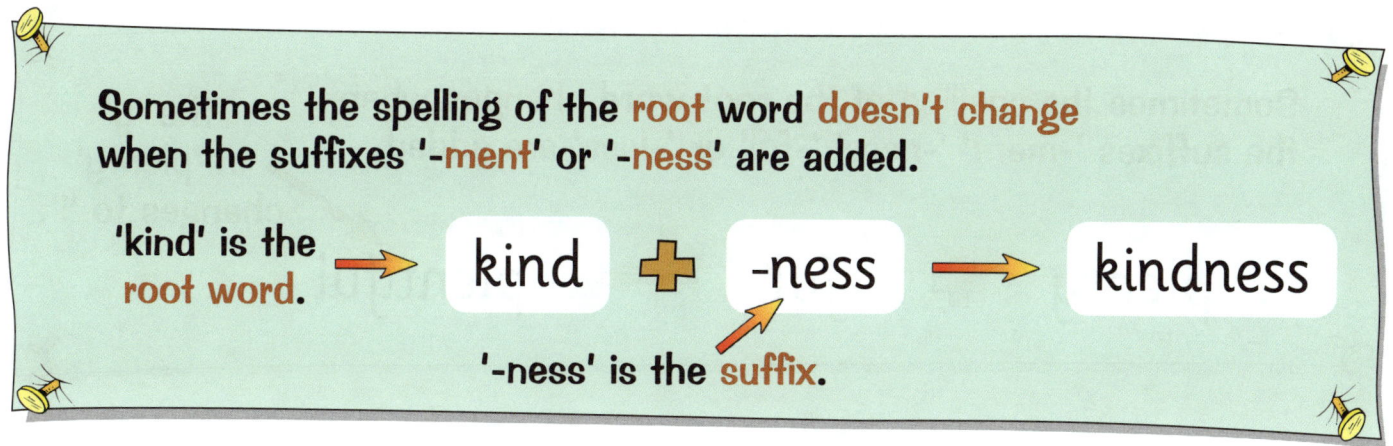

③ Shade in the words which use the correct suffix.

improve: improveness / improvement

bright: brightness / brightment

state: statement / stateness

mad: madment / madness

④ Draw lines to show which suffix should fill the gap in each sentence below.

I made a pay............ in the shop.

Lori had a bad ill............ .

Our fit............ is improving!

The move............ made me jump.

I couldn't see in the dark............ .

-ment

-ness

Sometimes the spelling of the root word changes when the suffixes '-ment' '-ness' '-ful' or '-less' are added.

The 'y' in 'plenty' changes to 'i'.

plenty + -ful → plent**i**ful

5 Shade the circles to show which underlined word is spelt correctly.

We had an argument. ○
We had an arguement. ○

She liked his tidiness. ○
She liked his tidyness. ○

Now he's pennyless. ○
Now he's penniless. ○

The view is beautyful. ○
The view is beautiful. ○

6 Add the suffixes to the root words to make new words.

pity + -less → ....

duty + -ful → ....

gloomy + -ness → ....

The underlined letters will change when the suffix is added.

7 Underline the correctly spelt words in each pair.

basement / basment   ugliness / uglyness

lazyness / laziness   graceful / gracful

Section 11 — Suffixes and Word Endings

Mixed Practice

Words can **end** in lots of different ways:

playing   **kick**ed   **waste**ful   **dark**est

Sometimes the spelling of the root word changes when suffixes are added.

ti**dy** → tid**iest**

1 Shade in the <u>correctly spelt</u> words below.

puncture   puncsure   expoture   exposure

leiture   leisure   moisture   moissure

2 Add each of the <u>four suffixes</u> to the <u>words</u> on the boards to create <u>new words</u>.

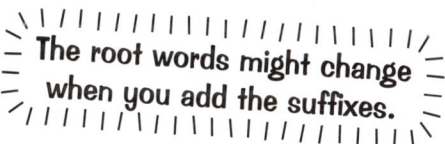
The root words might change when you add the suffixes.

 ~~ing~~   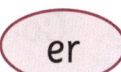 ed    er   ful

<u>play</u>
playing
....

....

....

....

<u>care</u>
caring
....

....

....

....

3) Circle the root words that change when '-ness' is added.

weak good lonely fair sloppy friendly

4) Write the name of the person who has spelt the underlined word correctly.

Erin — Happiness is important.

Fionn — Happyness is important.

.... has spelt the word correctly.

Aiko — I was the fastest runner.

Leilani — I was the fasttest runner.

.... has spelt the word correctly.

5) Use the clues to find the new words that are made when the suffix is added to the root word. Complete the crossword using the new words.

Across:
1. rise ➕ -ing
2. sail ➕ -ed

Down:
3. end ➕ -less
4. joy ➕ -ful

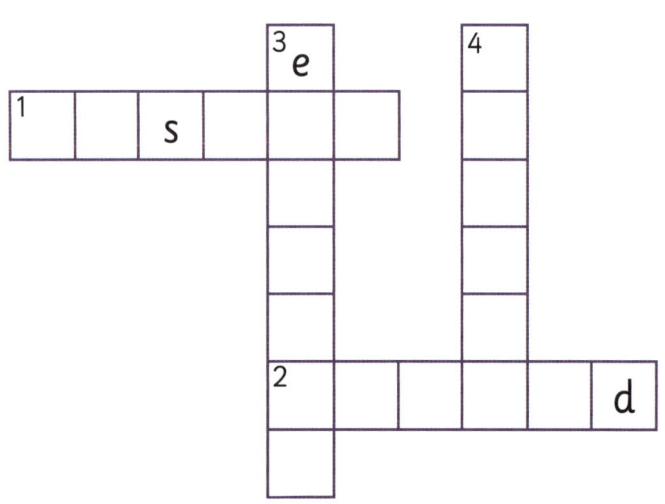

Section 12 — Confusing Words

The short 'i' sound

The short 'i' sound can be spelt with an i or a y.

tick   Egypt

1) Look at the pairs of words below. Tick the word that is spelt correctly.

mince ☐
mynce ☐

pynk ☐
pink ☐

simbol ☐
symbol ☐

2) Circle the correct spelling of each word to complete the sentences below.

She missed / myssed the bus.

He goes to the gim / gym.

The choir sings hymns / himns.

3) Fill in the boxes to correctly spell the words below. Use the picture clues to help you.

| k | n | | t |

| s | | r | u | p |

| w | | n | t | e | r |

The hard 'c' sound

The hard 'c' sound is like a 'k' sound.
Here are a few ways it can be spelt:

ba**c**k   **k**eep   **c**arrot

1) Draw lines to connect all the words with a hard 'c' sound to the balloon.

doctor   kind
    pack   hard 'c'
              sound   bear
                         topic
hand
                              purse

2) Look at the pairs of words below, then shade in the words that are spelt correctly.

snack   snak   walc   walk   kastle   castle

3) Read each sentence, then write the name of the person who has spelt the underlined word correctly.

Mischa   My aunt has a cuckoo clok.

Harun   I always worc very hard.

Lara   I bought a new camera.

.... has spelt the underlined word correctly.

Section 12 — Confusing Words

The soft 'c' sound

The soft 'c' sound is like an 's' sound.
Here are a couple of ways it can be spelt: seal   race

1 Circle the word in each pair that is spelt correctly.

sample / cample   sircle / circle

cement / sement   sencible / sensible

2 The soft 'c' sounds from the words below are missing.
Draw lines to match each word to the correct missing letter.

dan?e ——— s   repla?e   *The first one has been done for you.*
?imple   te?ting
li?ten   c   ?entre

3 Use the letters on the planets to make two words with the soft 'c' sound. Use the clues to help you.

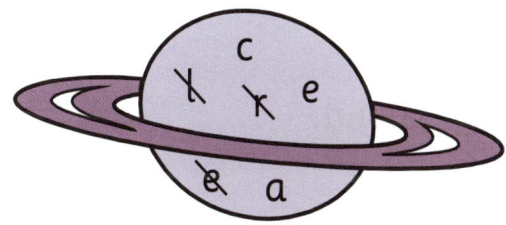
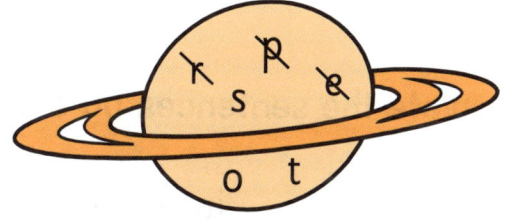

a food you eat with milk   something you put on a wall

| | | r | e | | l | | p | | | e | r |

The 'sh' sound

The 'sh' sound can be spelt in several different ways.

shed   **s**ugar   ma**ch**ine

1   Circle all the words that contain the '<u>sh</u>' sound.

shark	ache	mark	issue
swim	sure	shiny	dish

2   Rewrite the words below using the <u>correct spelling</u> of the '<u>sh</u>' sound.

champoo   **sh**ef   **s**ield

....

3   Complete the sentences by adding the '<u>sh</u>' sound.

The pirate ....ip disappeared.

Blow your nose with a ti........ue.

It's too cold to wear ....orts today.

The 'ay' sound

The 'ay' sound can be spelt in different ways.

pain   stay   male

1 Look at the pairs of words below, then shade in the words that are spelt correctly.

gayt   gate   nail   nale   trane   train

2 Fill in the missing letters to complete each word correctly. All the words have the 'ay' sound. Use the pictures to help you.

sn.........l

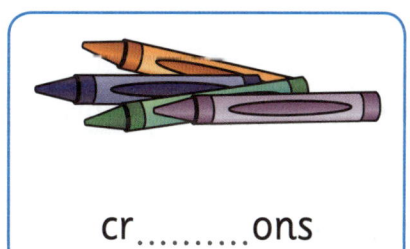
cr.........ons

spr.........

3 Complete the sentences below using the correct words from the box.

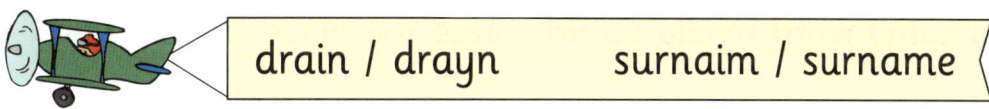
drain / drayn   surnaim / surname

Lisa spelt my .... wrong.

The leaves had blocked the ....

Word Families

Word families are groups of words that contain the same root. Their meanings are related — like a family.

unclean
cleaner   cleaning

All of these words contain the root 'clean'.

1 Look at these words belonging to the same word family. Underline the root for the family, then write it on the dotted line.

daylight   lightning   lighthouse

sunlight   moonlight   lightbulb

The root is ....

2 Tick the words that belong to the same word family as play.

player ☐   replay ☐   please ☐

angry ☐   playful ☐   delay ☐

3 Use the letters in the boxes to make two words that belong to the same word family as fire. Use the clues to help you.

f b n i o r e   y f f k k i e

a large fire you make outside   an insect which can create light

| b | | n | | i | | e |

| | i | r | | f | l | |

Section 12 — Confusing Words

Plurals

To make most words into **plurals**, add **s**.

car → car**s**

If a word ends in **ch**, **sh**, **s**, **ss**, **x** or **z**, add **es**.

wish → wish**es**

1 Look at the pairs of plural words below. Tick the words that are spelt <u>correctly</u>.

- melons ☐
- melones ☐

- birdes ☐
- birds ☐

- boxes ☐
- boxs ☐

- pathes ☐
- paths ☐

- dishs ☐
- dishes ☐

- herbs ☐
- herbes ☐

2 Complete the <u>table</u> below.

Word	Plural
shoe	....
thumb	....
dress	....
fox	....

For most words that end in **f**, change the **f** to a **v** and add **es**.

elf → el**ves**

For most words that end in **y**, change the **y** to **ies**.

fly → fl**ies**

3) Draw <u>lines</u> to match each word to the correct <u>plural ending</u>.

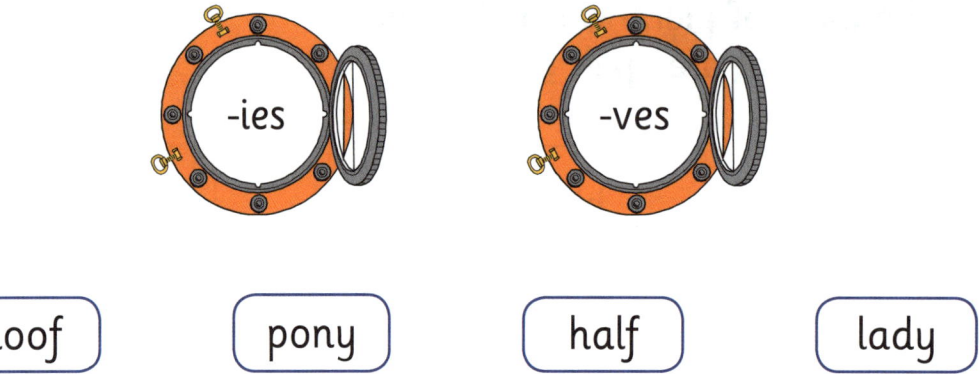

-ies   -ves

hoof   pony   half   lady

4) Complete the <u>crossword</u> with the <u>plural forms</u> of the words below. Some of the letters have been filled in for you.

1. baby   2. shelf   3. leaf   4. jelly

Section 12 — Confusing Words

Some **plurals** don't follow the rules. You just have to **learn** these.

fish → fish   man → men

foot → feet

5 Circle the <u>correct</u> spelling to complete each sentence.

The <u>sheeps</u> / <u>sheep</u> crossed the road.

I lost three <u>teeth</u> / <u>teeths</u> last week.

The <u>mouses</u> / <u>mice</u> ran away from the cat.

6 Complete the **plural** form of each of the words below.

moose → | m | | o | | e |

woman → | w | o | | | n |

person → | p | e | | p | l | |

7 Complete each sentence with the **plural** of the word in the box.

| plant | Remember to water the ....

| party | I don't like going to ....

| deer | There were some .... in the forest.

Homophones

Homophones are words that sound the same, but have different meanings and spellings.

shoe — Something you wear on your foot.

shoo — To scare something away.

1 Circle the correct word to describe each picture.

wheel   we'll

flower   flour

rose   rows

2 Shade in the word that is a homophone of the word on the left.

leek ⟶ seek   lock   leak

tail ⟶ tall   sail   tale

3 Circle the correct word to complete each sentence.

Dawud's favourite colour is blue / blew.

The son / sun was shining all day.

Sylvie helped me wrap / rap the present.

Section 12 — Confusing Words

4 Read each sentence, then write the name of the person who is correct.

- Uma — Buy and sky are homophones.
- Kylie — Been and bean are homophones.
- Austin — List and lost are homophones.

.... is correct.

5 Rearrange the letters to make homophones of the words below. The first letter of each word has been filled in for you.

e ~~h~~ l a	heel →	h ☐ ☐ ☐
o ~~s~~ r e	saw →	s ☐ ☐ ☐
a d e ~~r~~	reed →	r ☐ ☐ ☐
e ~~w~~ k e	weak →	w ☐ ☐ ☐

6 Write the homophone that matches each picture.

source → ....

wail → ....

Mixed Practice

1) Shade in the words that belong to the same <u>word family</u> as <u>life</u>.

breathe   wildlife   lifestyle   wife   lifeboat

2) Draw lines to match the pairs of <u>homophones</u>.

four   main   sole

for   soul   mane

3) Read each sentence, then write the <u>name</u> of the person who is <u>correct</u>.

Linus   The word 'prince' has a short 'i' sound.

Neave   The word 'island' has a short 'i' sound.

Ralph   The word 'piece' has a short 'i' sound.

.... is correct.

4) Circle the <u>correct</u> spelling of each word to complete the sentences.

What is the prise / price of this T-shirt?

It was their last chance / chanse to escape.

Shelby is a cerious / serious person.

Section 12 — Confusing Words

5) Put a <u>tick</u> in the boxes next to the words that have the <u>hard 'c'</u> sound.

dice ☐   kettle ☐   charm ☐   course ☐

6) Shade in the word that is the <u>plural</u> of the word on the left.

kite → kites kities kives

penny → pennys pennies pennyes

wolf → wolvs wolves wolfs

7) Draw lines to match each word to its <u>missing letters</u>.

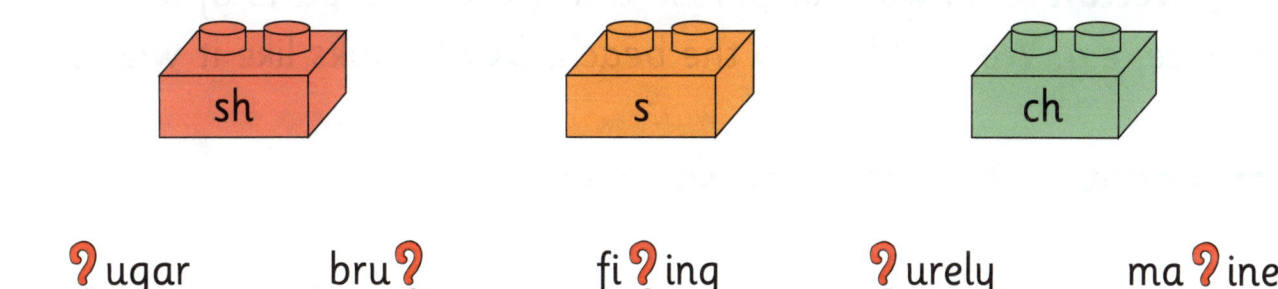

?ugar   bru?   fi?ing   ?urely   ma?ine

8) Complete the words with an '<u>ay</u>' sound. Use the pictures to help you.

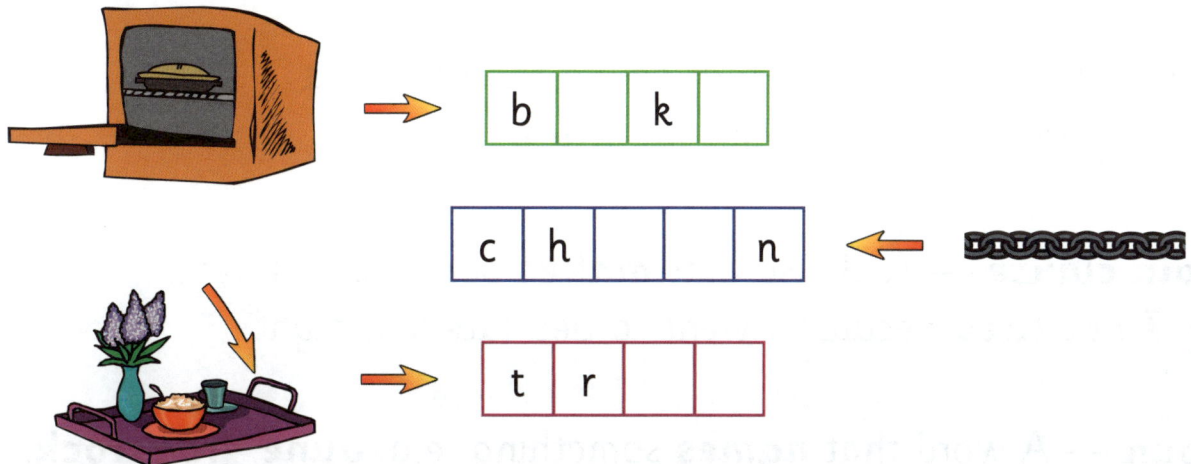

b ☐ k ☐

c h ☐ ☐ n

t r ☐ ☐

Glossary

Adjective — A word that describes a noun, e.g. **red** nose.

Adverb — A word that describes a verb, e.g. run **quickly**.

Article — The words **a**, **an** and **the**.

Clause — Part of a sentence that normally contains a **subject** (**someone** or **something** doing the action) and a **verb**.

Command — A sentence that gives an **instruction** or an **order**, e.g. **Eat your dinner!**

Conjunction — A word or phrase that **joins** two parts of a sentence, e.g. We could go to the beach, **but** it looks like it will rain.

Consonant — Any letter that **isn't** a vowel.

Exclamation — A sentence that shows **strong feelings**, beginning with '**how**' or '**what**', e.g. **What a wonderful surprise this is!**

Heading — Tells you the **main topic** of a text.

Homophones — Words that sound the same but have different **spellings** and **meanings**.

Main clause — A clause that **makes sense** on its own. e.g. **I am tired** because I went to bed late last night.

Noun — A word that **names** something, e.g. **June, frog, rock**.

Glossary

Paragraph — A **group of sentences** about the same **time**, **person** or **subject**.

Phrase — A group of words usually without a **verb**.

Prefix — Letters that can be put **in front** of a word to change its **meaning**, e.g. **re**place.

Preposition — Tells you **where**, **when** or **why** something happens.

Question — A sentence that tries to **find out information**, e.g. **What's the time?**

Statement — A sentence that **tells you something**, e.g. **The door is open**.

Subheading — Tells you the topic of **smaller sections** within a text.

Suffix — Letters that can be put **after** a word to change its **meaning**, e.g. bright**est**.

Verb — A doing or being word, e.g. **bury**, **speaks**, **hear**, **am**.

Vowel — The letters **a**, **e**, **i**, **o**, **u** and **sometimes y**.

Word family — A **group** of words that contain the **same root**. Their meanings are related, e.g. child<u>care</u>, <u>care</u>ful, <u>care</u>less.

Glossary

COMMON PUNCTUATION MARKS

Apostrophes — show **missing letters** and **possession**.   **'**

Capital letters — used for **starting** sentences and for **names** or **I**.   **A**

Commas — used to separate **items** in a **list**.   **,**

Exclamation marks — show **strong emotions** or **commands**.   **!**

Full stops — show where **sentences end**.   **.**

Inverted commas — show when someone is **speaking**. They can also be called '**speech marks**'.   **" "**

Question marks — used at the **end** of **questions**.   **?**

Answers

Grammar

Section 1 — Word Types

Page 4 — Nouns

1. You should have matched these nouns and pictures:

   apple   spoon   snake   bird

2. You should have shaded: April, Friday, Scotland, Chester.

Page 5 — Adjectives

1. You should have matched the following adjectives to the pictures:

    dirty, pink, happy
    grey, fluffy, angry

2. You should have underlined:
   a <u>good</u> book, the <u>spotty</u> pants, a <u>small</u> dog, the <u>big</u> lizard, a <u>hungry</u> horse, a <u>green</u> door, the <u>sad</u> shark, the <u>sticky</u> floor.

Pages 6 and 7 — Articles

1. You should have circled the words in bold:
   I found **an** ant.
   Malika has **a** garden.
   This is **an** otter.
   We saw **a** zebra.

2. You should have shaded: There is an elephant.

3. You should have matched:
   a: girl, bee, rainbow, flower
   an: umbrella, oven, arrow

4. You should have ticked:
   the party
   an orange
   the day
   a gift

5. **an** owl, **the** frog

6. You should have circled the words in bold:
   I spoke to her on **the** phone.
   Thailand is **a** country in Asia.
   This film is **the** best!

Pages 8 and 9 — Verbs

1. You should have matched these verbs and pictures:

   sing   kick   jump   drink

2. You should have shaded: eat, speak, hear, know.

3. You should have ticked:
   They <u>like</u> kittens.
   He <u>screams</u>.

4. You should have matched:
   play: I, they, you
   plays: Boris, the boy, she

5. You should have circled the words in bold:
   You **listen**.
   I **am** happy.
   We **see** Grandma.
   Magda **loves** animals.
   He **wins** the prize.

6. You should have circled the words in bold:
   He **swims**.
   I **talk** to them.
   She **lives** here.
   We **go** to the park.
   He **buys** a guitar.
   She **paints**.

Pages 10 and 11 — Adverbs

1. adverbs: sadly, angrily, usually, badly

2. You should have ticked:
   The fox moved <u>sneakily</u>.
   The bell rang <u>suddenly</u>.
   Maria <u>never</u> washes up.

3. The mouse moved silently. — **how**
   We are leaving today. — **when**
   I clean my shoes sometimes. — **how often**

4. You should have underlined:
   He skips <u>happily</u>.
   She <u>always</u> forgets.
   They ask <u>nervously</u>.
   Erin <u>often</u> smiles.
   We will go <u>soon</u>.
   It walks <u>slowly</u>.

5. She runs **quickly**.
   The sun shines **brightly**.

Answers

Pages 12 and 13 — Mixed Practice

1. You should have shaded:

   angry   pretty   happy

2. verb: bury, write, learn, speak
   noun: muffin, lizard, chess, sandal

3. You should have shaded: I walked in the afternoon.

4. The dog growls **loudly**.
   The man looks **closely**.
   The woman dresses **smartly**.

5. He is next to the **plant**.
   He is wearing **a** hat.
   He is holding **an** umbrella.

Section 2 — Clauses, Phrases and Sentences

Page 14 — Clauses

1. You should have ticked: the girls skipped, Bella giggled.

2. You should have matched these pairs:
   He was happy — because it was sunny.
   I went home — once I'd finished shopping.
   She stayed up — until her parents arrived.

3. You should have written 'M' next to:
   <u>I will sing</u> if everyone listens.

Page 15 — Phrases

1. You should have shaded: very smelly, next to me.

2. You should have ticked: a large crocodile, with a fierce grin.

3. Henna hid **before the show**.
   The vase shattered **into tiny pieces**.
   Dad ate the **lemon cupcakes**.

Pages 16 and 17 — Statements and Questions

1. You should have ticked:
   It was hot on safari.
   The boys were shouting.
   I don't know where it is.
   Mum's car is bright red.

2. You should have shaded:
   Is someone there?
   Is it strawberry?
   Can I have a go?

3. You should have matched these pairs:
   What time is it? — It is 5 o'clock.
   Where is your shirt? — It's in my wardrobe.
   How much is it? — It is fifty pounds.

4. Any suitable answers.
   Examples:
   Is he friendly?
   Am I noisy?
   You are busy.
   The soup is hot.

5. Any suitable answers.
   Examples:
   statement: **She is cooking pizza.**
   question: **Is she cooking pizza?**

Pages 18 and 19 — Commands and Exclamations

1. You should have shaded:
   How loud that music is!
   What a small kitten that is!
   What long hair you have!

2. You should have ticked:
   Close the kitchen window.
   Take your sister to the park.
   Wash your hands now.

3. How polite you are! — **exclamation**
   Put away your clothes. — **command**
   What a tasty meal that was! — **exclamation**
   Stir the mixture carefully. — **command**

4. **Callum** has written an exclamation.

5. **Water the flowers.**
   How thirsty I am!

Pages 20 and 21 — Mixed Practice

1. You should have ticked:
   in the way
   out of the box
   too salty
   the old cleaner

2. Is she going to help? — **question**
   I don't like vegetables. — **statement**
   They went to the cinema. — **statement**
   Why are you talking? — **question**

Answers

3. in the morning — **phrase**
   We ate breakfast — **main clause**
   He wiped his nose — **main clause**
   between us — **phrase**
   to the fair — **phrase**

4. What lovely flowers they are! — **exclamation**
   Stop chasing the rabbit. — **command**
   Leave the milk out for me. — **command**
   How exciting this is! — **exclamation**

5. Any suitable main clause.
   Example:
   The donkey ate

Section 3 — Conjunctions and Prepositions

Pages 22 and 23 — Conjunctions

1. You should have shaded: so, and, but, or.

2. You should have ticked:
   He didn't go outside, for it was raining.

3. You should have underlined:
   The tiger roared, <u>so</u> the deer ran away.
   I can wash the dishes, <u>or</u> I can sweep the floor.
   She wore blue socks with red stripes, <u>yet</u> no one noticed.

4. You should have matched these conjunctions and clauses:
   The rabbit ate the carrot, — and — **it bit my finger.**
   It had snowed, — so — **it was cold outside.**
   I knew it was wrong, — but — **I still stole the pencil.**

5. I was very tired, **but** I didn't go to bed.

6. The horse jumped over the gate, **and** it ran away.
   I will bake a cake, **or** I will make a pie.
   His shoes were dirty, **so** he had to clean them.

Pages 24 and 25 — Prepositions

1. You should have ticked:
   The hat is on Mei's head.
   The bird is behind the tree.
   The fish is in the bowl.

2. Jacob drew a picture after school. — **when**
   Your shoes are in the hallway. — **where**
   There were trees between the buildings. — **where**
   I heard a noise during the night. — **when**

3. **Stevie** uses the correct preposition.

4. You should have circled the words in bold:
   The cat jumped **onto** the sofa.
   I took some sweets **from** the bowl.
   Nicole saw Tahani **on** the bus.
   Please take the rubbish **outside** the house.

5. Any suitable answer.
   Examples:
   The rat is **inside** the purse.
   The bird is **above** the clouds.

Section 4 — Verb Tenses

Pages 26 and 27 — Present and Past Tense — Regular Verbs

1. You should have underlined: <u>skip</u>, <u>pat</u>, <u>jump</u>, <u>shout</u>.

2. Present tense: look, closes, crush, date
   Past tense: looked, closed, crushed, dated

3. use + d = used
   fold + **ed** = **folded**
   age + **d** = **aged**
   dress + **ed** = **dressed**

4. I **walked** my dog.
   Brooke **cooked** dinner.
   We **picked** some flowers.

5.
present tense	past tense
I chase him.	I chased him.
Malik cleans.	Malik cleaned.
Belle climbs.	Belle climbed.

Pages 28 and 29 — Present and Past Tense — Irregular Verbs

1. You should have matched these verbs:
   catch — caught
   makes — made
   keeps — kept
   sleep — slept

2. It **sang**. They **drink**. He **saw**. She **rides**.

3. **had, fell, left, grew**

o	r	m	h	n	g
e	h	a	d	l	r
t	g	w	p	a	e
l	e	f	t	s	w
a	c	v	o	h	i
d	r	f	e	l	l

Answers

4. You should have circled the words in bold:
   I **knew** it was going to rain.
   Robin **heard** the loud party.
   We **began** our lessons.
   A helicopter **flew** over our house.
   Eric **gave** Diego a biscuit.

5. I **ring** my grandma.
   Rory **says** goodbye.
   Fleur **gets** paid.

Pages 30 and 31 — Staying in the Same Tense

1. You should have matched:
   I went shopping — and bought milk.
   I like carrots — but I hate peas.
   I hid quietly — then jumped out.

2. I chose the colours when we **painted** my room.
   Ellie **writes** poetry and draws pictures.
   Caleb wrapped the gift and **wrote** in the card.
   Our teacher lets us **paint** during art lessons.

3. You should have circled the words in bold:
   Today I **visited** the zoo, and I saw a lion.
   My mum **takes** the biscuits, and she eats them secretly.
   Ajani went to the beach, and he **got** an ice cream.

4. I cook, **clean** and watch TV.
   Veena **feels** happy, so she smiles.
   He hates art, but he **loves** maths.
   We whisked, **baked** then ate.

5. The suspect broke into the safe and **stole** the diamond. Unfortunately, nobody saw where the man **went**.

Punctuation

Section 5 — Sentence Punctuation

Pages 32 and 33 — Capital Letters for Names and I

1. Name of a person: Michael, Sally
   Name of a month: September, November
   Name of a place: Scotland, Wales

2. You should have circled: france, katie, monday.
   You should have rewritten: **France**, **Katie**, **Monday**.

3. You should have shaded: Norway is next to Sweden.

4. You should have ticked: I bought a house in China.

5. You should have circled the words in bold:
   My birthday is in **December**.
   Eliza's favourite colour is **purple**.
   I met our new neighbour called Ying.

6. **I** live in **Cornwall**.
   It's sunny in **August**.
   Windsor Castle is old.
   I saw **Isabelle**.

Pages 34 and 35 — Capital Letters and Full Stops

1. My pencil broke — **full stop**
   Our plants grew — **full stop**
   luka is late. — **capital letter**
   pass the milk. — **capital letter**
   the sun is setting. — **capital letter**
   I'm going out — **full stop**

2. Haley ran a race. She won a medal.
   I got a new bike. It is blue.
   The party was fun. It was loud.
   I love puppies. They are cute.

3. You should have circled: i, her, lola, she.

4. I'm very tired. **I'm** going to bed.
   Carrots are a vegetable.
   Pugs are nice dogs.
   It was really cold. **It** snowed.

5. **Leo** came round to my house.
   I was reading my **book**.
   My football match is today.

6. **The frog is wearing flippers.**

Pages 36 and 37 — Question Marks

1. You should have circled: why, what, how, where, when, who.

2. What time should we leave — **question mark**
   Charlie is playing a chess game — **full stop**
   Tortoises have very hard shells — **full stop**
   Why is everyone wearing green — **question mark**

3. Who is that woman**?**
   My birthday is tomorrow**.**
   Where was the party**?**
   That was a nice surprise**.**
   When are you free**?**
   How was your day**?**
   The hamster is small**.**
   I made a plan**.**

4. When: is it ready?, did it happen?, can I go?
   Who: did it?, called me?, was there?

Answers

5. Any sentence which begins with a capital letter and matches the answer.
   Example:
   Where is the hat?
   What time is it?

Pages 38 and 39 — Exclamation Marks

1. You should have ticked:
   The shop is giving away free sweets!
   They are making so much noise!

2. You should have matched:
   Greg made a cup of tea — .
   We are going to be so late — !
   The sheep are in the field — .
   All the money has been stolen — !

3. Wow, your hair is huge**!**
   I like music**.**
   Ed is watching TV**.**
   Look, it's lightning**!**

4. You should have underlined:
   It's broken
   She was horrid
   Get set, go

5. Yesterday was boring **.** Today was very exciting**!**
   Kylie is learning Spanish**.** It is really difficult**!**
   A gigantic storm hit the island**!** The next day it was calm**.**

Pages 40 and 41 — Sentence Practice

1. You should have shaded:
   Where are we?
   Hurry up!
   Why me?
   I know.

2. I have two rabbits. — **no capital letter**
   The aliens are from jupiter. — **capital letter**
   Gabby likes vanilla ice cream. — **no capital letter**
   There are mountains in ireland. — **capital letter**

3. You should have ticked:
   How is it made?
   The volcano is erupting!

4. You should have underlined:
   Nikko's family are from japan.
   i rang Whitney while I was walking home.
   My neighbour sheila has spiders in her porch.
   Shreya received flowers for her birthday in may.
   We are going on a trip to wales!

5.

	.	!	?
Chloe lives in Brazil	(.)	!	?
The curry is too hot	.	(!)	?
Which colour would you like	.	!	(?)
The grass is green	(.)	!	?

6. **W**hich one is it**?**

Section 6 — Commas

Pages 42 and 43 — Writing Lists

1. He hates cats, dogs and rabbits. — **uses commas correctly**
   He hates cats, dogs and, rabbits. — **uses commas incorrectly**
   She could make, pizza, pasta or soup. — **uses commas incorrectly**
   She could make pizza, pasta or soup. — **uses commas correctly**

2. They skipped, smiled **and** laughed.
   I told Jenny**,** Niles and Wesley.
   Do you want water, juice **or** squash?

3. You should have circled the commas in bold:
   Shall we order**,** burgers, chips or ice cream?
   The weather is clear, sunny and**,** hot.
   The zoo**,** has elephants, tigers and monkeys.

4. You should have shaded:
   I play tennis, rugby, football and hockey.

5. We need pens, pencils and rubbers.
   The farmer owns pigs**,** sheep and goats.
   Amira isn't greedy**,** mean or nasty.

6. Any suitable answer that uses the words from the boxes.
   Example:
   We saw **ducks**, **cows** and **pigs**.

Pages 44 and 45 — Writing Longer Lists

1. You should have ticked:
   We sold the sparkly shoes, the gold tiara and the dress.
   He found a broken watch, a pair of gloves and a wallet.

Answers

2. You should have circled the commas in bold:
   There were yellow daffodils, red tulips and white daisies**,** in her garden.
   They peeled the potatoes, chopped the carrots and**,** crushed the garlic.
   I went swimming with Felix, played netball and rode**,** my bike.

3. **Kabir** uses commas correctly.

4. I don't watch TV**,** listen to music or play games.
   She gave me some biscuits**,** a jar of jam and a box of eggs.
   I want chocolate buttons**,** jelly beans and gummy bears.
   The shop had no red grapes**,** green peppers or brown bread.

5. She bought a cowboy hat**,** a red belt and a loaf of bread.

Section 7 — Apostrophes

Pages 46 and 47 — Apostrophes for Missing Letters

1. You should have shaded: I'm, he'll, you're, they've.

2. You should have matched:
   he is — he's
   I have — I've
   you will — you'll

3. You should have crossed out these letters to make the shortened words:
   did n̶o̶t̶ — **didn't**
   was n̶o̶t̶ — **wasn't**
   that i̶s̶ — **that's**
   it w̶ill — **it'll**

4. **We are**
   do not

5. **hasn't**
   she'd
   doesn't
   they're

Pages 48 and 49 — Its and It's

1. You should have ticked:
   It's sunny.
   It's Friday.
   It's almost Christmas.
   It's red and white.

2. You should have shaded: The shop closed its doors.

3. **It's** dark.
   It's snowed.
   It's Tuesday.

4. You should have ticked:
   It's very cold outside.
   The puppy wagged its tail.

5. It's been lovely. — **it has**
   It's raining. — **it is**
   It's pretty. — **it is**
   It's fallen over. — **it has**

6. **It's** three o'clock in the afternoon.
   The cat carried the kitten in **its** mouth.
   The bear sleeps in **its** cave.
   Thank you, **it's** just what I wanted.

Pages 50 and 51 — Apostrophes for Single Possession

1. Fiona**'s** jumper.
   Dad**'s** name.
   The boy**'s** room.
   The snake**'s** scales.

2. It's **Sandy's** book.
   It's **Esme's** cat.

3. You should have ticked:
   Carys's lemons
   Eric's holiday
   Taylor's pencil
   Angus's cousin
   the boss's office

4. Any answers that use apostrophes correctly.
   Example:
   Hardeep's strawberry
   Abigail's football
   Thomas's dog
   Nia's armchair

Pages 52 and 53 — Apostrophe Practice

1. the goat's horns
   the walrus's tusks
   James's picture

2.

Long version	Shortened version
Where is the party?	Where's the party?
We have been outside.	We've been outside.
I am Rina.	**I'm** Rina.
That is a loud noise.	That's a loud noise.
Ethan does not shout.	Ethan **doesn't** shout.

Answers

3. You should have put a cross next to:
   The mans' shoes are brown.

4. Esther <u>can't</u> go — **for missing letters**
   <u>Noah's</u> brother — **to show possession**
   the <u>girl's</u> eyes — **to show possession**
   <u>we'll</u> see you — **for missing letters**

5. You should have shaded: Louis's pen

6. **It's** really scary.
   Its fur is purple.
   It's got big feet.

Section 8 — Inverted Commas

Pages 54 and 55 — Inverted Commas

1. **Leon** uses inverted commas correctly.

2. You should have crossed out the inverted commas in bold:
   "This is delicious!" said Nadine**"**.
   "Where is the ball?" **"**asked Romeo.
   "Come back **"**later, " said Zehra.
   "Thank you!" said Harry**."**
   "Is that**"** the time?" asked Laurie.

3. You should have ticked:
   "I want to be a teacher," said Dan.
   "Would you like a biscuit?" asked Alvin.

4. "Where are we going?" asked Daisy.
   "It's a lovely day," said Ansh.
   "I don't want to go to bed!" said Damien.
   "There are fish in the river," said Siobhan.

5. "Goodbye!" said **Kat**.
   "What time?" asked **Sam**.

Pages 56 to 58 — Punctuating Speech

1. What shall we eat?" — **inverted comma**
   "it's getting late." — **capital letter**
   "The film was great! — **inverted comma**
   "how do you feel?" — **capital letter**
   Laura is ill today." — **inverted comma**
   "hide quickly!" — **capital letter**

2. You should have ticked:
   "<u>do</u> you have a middle name?" asked Sheng.
   "<u>we</u> don't know where we are!" cried Livia.

3. "**Throw** the ball!" cried Tinaye.
   "Where are you?" **asked** Ryan.
   Fran asked, "Do you **like** it?"
   Finn shouted, "**I** can see you!"

4. "**Whales** live in the sea," said Omari.
   Libby said, "**Well** done everyone!"
   "**Have** you seen my glasses?" asked Pat.

5. You should have shaded:
   "We are getting a new pet," said Tory.
   "I get my pocket money soon," said Nisha.

6. You should have circled the words in bold:
   "**the** music is too loud!" shouted Jia.
   Cameron said, "**please** close the door."
   "**i** want to play the guitar," said Ariana.

7. Any suitable answers.
   Examples:
   "You're welcome," I said.
   Lee cried, "They're here!"
   "How many?" I asked.

8. You should have ticked:
   "Do you want to stay over?" asked Eshal.
   Holly said, "I'm moving to the seaside!"
   Alice asked, "Have you washed my top?"
   You should have rewritten:
   "I cycle to work every day," said Dylan.

Section 9 — Paragraphs and Layout

Pages 59 and 60 — Paragraphs

1. You should have shaded:
   They start on a new line.
   They group sentences about the same things together.
   They make your writing easier to read.

2. You should have ticked:
   When you write about a different subject.
   When you write about a different time.
   When you write about a new person.

3. You should have matched these sentences together:
   I made a necklace at the weekend. — The beads are red and purple.
   We are going on holiday next week. — I really hope it doesn't rain.

4. I love dogs. They're very friendly and soft. My dog is called Spot. — **subject**
   My sister is three years older than me. She has brown hair and green eyes. — **person**

5. I want to be a doctor when I grow up. I want to help make people better. // My brother is a doctor. He works in a hospital.
   You should have circled: **new person**

Answers

Page 61 — Headings and Subheadings

1. **Henry** is correct.

2. **Main text** — Come along and discover our prehistoric giants. Opens on 27th January.
   Heading — NEW MUSEUM DISPLAY
   Subheading — Prehistoric Giants

Spelling
Section 10 — Prefixes

Pages 62 and 63 — Prefixes — 'un' 'dis' and 'mis'

1. mis-: treat, match, shape
   dis-: obey, own, allow

2. You should have circled: even, kind, true.
   You should have written: un**even**, **un**kind, **un**true.

3.

Prefix	Root word	New word
dis-	grace	disgrace
un-	well	unwell
mis-	time	mistime
un-	made	unmade

4. **dis**agree, **mis**read, **un**wrap

5. Raheem's bedroom is un**tidy**.
   I dis**approve** of the new rules.
   The newspaper mis**printed** my name.

Page 64 — Prefixes — 're' and 'anti'

1. You should have shaded: replay, antivirus, antisocial, restart.

2. **anti**biotic, **anti**climax, **re**fill, **re**view

   ```
   r x a e t (r) x t m i
   a (r e v i e w) w a f
   x n i r b f i w x e
   (a n t i b i o t i c)
   i b r w n l b e r b
   (a n t i c l i m a x)
   ```

Page 65 — Prefixes — 'sub' and 'super'

1. **super**glue, **sub**merge

2. sub-: way, marine
   super-: model, power

Pages 66 and 67 — Mixed Practice

1. refund, **antiseptic**, **replace**, **antifreeze**

2. **Tai** is using the correct prefix.
   Kelly is using the correct prefix.

3. You should have put a cross next to:
   The team are antibeaten this year.

4. I never **mis**behave in lessons.
   My last biscuit has **dis**appeared.
   There are two **sub**headings in the article.

5. You should have matched:
   super — hero
   un — happy
   dis — order
   You should have written the words beneath these pictures:

superhero   **unhappy**   **disorder**

Section 11 — Suffixes and Word Endings

Pages 68 and 69 — Word Endings — 'sure' and 'ture'

1. -sure: compo-, expo-
   -ture: sculp-, depar-

2. You should have circled: mois-, fu-, pic-.
   You should have written: **mois**ture, **fu**ture, **pic**ture.

3. m**ature**, trea**sure**

4. The lion's **enclosure**.
   The **structure** was huge!
   It's a scary **creature**.
   We go to the **leisure** centre.

5. It's a plea**sure** to meet you!
   She's going on an adven**ture**.
   We are buying furni**ture**.
   Let's mea**sure** your height.

6. She stirred the **mixture**.
   Cruz got a book about **nature**.

Answers

Pages 70 and 71 — Suffixes — 'ing' and 'ed'

1.

Root word	Add -ing	Add -ed
jump	jumping	**jumped**
hook	**hooking**	hooked
peek	**peeking**	**peeked**
fix	fixing	**fixed**

2. **boiling**, **mixed**
   1. Stir until the ingredients are **mixed** together.
   2. Make sure the water is **boiling**.

3. You should have shaded:
   tidied, spotted, scraping, saving.

4. The film was **boring**.
   Peter **copied** my homework!
   He **tripped** over his shoelace.

5. **flipping**, **buried**

Pages 72 and 73 — Suffixes — 'er' and 'est'

1. light — lighter   light — lightest
   loud — loud**er**   loud — loud**est**
   great — great**er** great — great**est**

2. short, short**er**, short**est**
   long, long**er**, long**est**

3. The dog is **friendlier** than the cat.
   I am a very safe **driver**.
   Lorenzo's costume was the **creepiest**.

4. closer, **closest**
   crazier, craziest
   thinner, **thinnest**

5. She is a police **officer**.
   I want a **fancier** hat.

Pages 74 to 76 — Suffixes — 'ful' 'less' 'ment' and 'ness'

1. use, **use**ful, **use**less
   help, **helpful**, **helpless**
   harm, **harmful**, **harmless**

2. The painting looked **flaw**less.
   The quiet park was **peace**ful.

3. You should have shaded: improvement, brightness, statement, madness.

4. I made a pay**ment** in the shop.
   Lori had a bad ill**ness**.
   Our fit**ness** is improving!
   The move**ment** made me jump.
   I couldn't see in the dark**ness**.

5. You should have shaded the circles next to:
   We had an argument.
   She liked his tidiness.
   Now he's penniless.
   The view is beautiful.

6. **pitiless**, **dutiful**, **gloominess**

7. You should have underlined: basement, laziness, ugliness, graceful.

Pages 77 and 78 — Mixed Practice

1. You should have shaded: puncture, leisure, exposure, moisture.

2. playing, **played**, **player**, **playful**
   caring, **cared**, **carer**, **careful**

3. You should have circled: sloppy, lonely, friendly.

4. **Erin** has spelt the word correctly.
   Aiko has spelt the word correctly.

5.

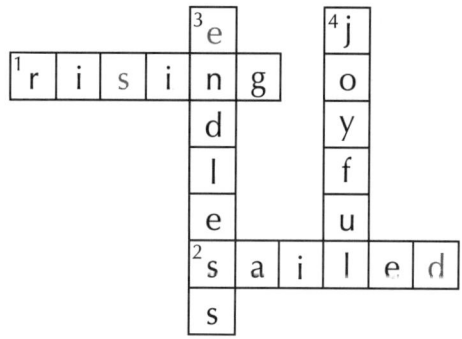

Section 12 — Confusing Words

Page 79 — The short 'i' sound

1. You should have ticked: mince, pink, symbol.

2. You should have circled the words in bold:
   She **missed** the bus.
   He goes to the **gym**.
   The choir sings **hymns**.

3. kn**i**t, s**y**rup, w**i**nter

Page 80 — The hard 'c' sound

1. hard 'c' sound: doctor, pack, kind, topic.

2. You should have shaded: snack, walk, castle.

3. **Lara** has spelt the underlined word correctly.

Answers

Page 81 — The soft 'c' sound

1. You should have circled: sample, circle, cement, sensible.

2. 's': **s**imple, li**s**ten, te**s**ting
   'c': dan**c**e, repla**c**e, **c**entre

3. **ce**real, po**s**ter

Page 82 — The 'sh' sound

1. You should have circled: shark, sure, shiny, issue, dish.

2. **sh**ampoo, **ch**ef, **sh**ield

3. The pirate **sh**ip disappeared.
   Blow your nose with a ti**ss**ue.
   It's too cold to wear **sh**orts today.

Page 83 — The 'ay' sound

1. You should have shaded: gate, nail, train.

2. sn**ai**l, cr**ay**ons, spr**ay**

3. Lisa spelt my **surname** wrong.
   The leaves had blocked the **drain**.

Page 84 — Word Families

1. day<u>light</u>, <u>light</u>ning, <u>light</u>house,
   sun<u>light</u>, moon<u>light</u>, <u>light</u>bulb
   The root is **light**.

2. You should have ticked: player, replay, playful.

3. b**on**fire, fir**efl**y

Pages 85 to 87 — Plurals

1. You should have ticked: melons, paths, birds, dishes, boxes, herbs.

2.

Word	Plural
shoe	shoes
thumb	thumbs
dress	dresses
fox	foxes

3. -ies: pony, lady
   -ves: hoof, half

4.

					¹b
²s	³h	e	l	v	e	s	a
	e				b
	a				i
	v				e
⁴j	e	l	l	i	e	s
	s				

5. You should have circled the words in bold:
   The **sheep** crossed the road.
   I lost three **teeth** last week.
   The **mice** ran away from the cat.

6. m**oo**se, w**o**men, pe**op**l**e**

7. Remember to water the **plants**.
   I don't like going to **parties**.
   There were some **deer** in the forest.

Pages 88 and 89 — Homophones

1. You should have circled: wheel, flour, rose.

2. You should have shaded: leak, tale.

3. You should have circled the words in bold:
   Dawud's favourite colour is **blue**.
   The **sun** was shining all day.
   Sylvie helped me **wrap** the present.

4. **Kylie** is correct.

5. h**eal**, s**o**re, r**ea**d, w**ee**k

6. **sauce**, **whale**

Pages 90 and 91 — Mixed Practice

1. You should have shaded: wildlife, lifestyle, lifeboat.

2. You should have matched these pairs:
   four — for, main — mane, sole — soul

3. **Linus** is correct.

4. You should have circled the words in bold:
   What is the **price** of this T-shirt?
   It was their last **chance** to escape.
   Shelby is a **serious** person.

5. You should have ticked: kettle, course.

6. You should have shaded: kites, pennies, wolves.

7. sh: bru**sh**, fi**sh**ing
   s: **s**ugar, **s**urely
   ch: ma**ch**ine

8. b**a**ke, ch**ai**n, tr**ay**